Franciscan Footprints

Book I
Pilgrimage to Assisi
Book II
Forth From the Garden
Second Edition

GLORIA PEARSON-VASEY, ofs

BY THE SAME AUTHOR

RED APPLE
PUBLISHING

CONTENTS

ACKNOWLEDGMENTS

This book is a tribute to Brother Alan Goebel, OFM Cap., our dedicated, knowledgeable and nurturing guide who led us through the hill towns, caves and cloisters of Umbria, to Anna, Virginia and Jim who generously shared their personal journaling, and to all the pilgrims who accompanied us on our spiritual quest in the footsteps of Francis and Clare of Assisi.

.

BOOK I
Pilgrimage to Assisi

We are spouses, when by the Holy Spirit the faithful soul is united with our Lord Jesus Christ, we are brothers to him when we fulfill "the will of the Father who is in heaven". We are mothers, when we carry him in our heart and body through divine love and a pure and sincere conscience; we give birth to him through a holy life which must give light to others by example.

Introduction

In September 2002, my husband, Jim, and I were among fourteen pilgrims led by capuchin friar, Brother Alan Gaebel, to the land dear to the hearts of Saints Francis and Clare.

Jim and I had been to Assisi previously and have returned since, but this particular pilgrimage was different from the others. Brother Alan was revisiting the sites he had seen in 1999, prior to making his final vows, and he wanted us to share his joy as he retraced his steps.

Thus we were privileged to tour caves, chapels,

monasteries and cloisters inaccessible to most pilgrims. We visited the caves and hermitages of the Carceri on Mount Subasio, the tiny Leper Church near Rivo Torto, the hermitages at La Celle and Monte Cassale, the ancient corridors and cloisters of the Sacro Convento adjoining the Basilica of San Francesco.

Moreover, we were able to stay in Assisi itself for ten amazing days, using the holy city as the base for our day trips to sacred sites cherished by Francis, Clare and their companions. Housed at St. Anthony's Guesthouse, we prayed, shared our experiences, and enjoyed the warm hospitality of the Franciscan Sisters of Atonement.

Appendix I contains the pilgrimage notes of Brother Alan, Jim, *Anna and Virginia*, who consented to share their journals (with the latter two choosing to remain anonymous). It also includes selected *Franciscan Readings*, required study by our enthusiastic guide.

The following word images and photographs attempt to capture the essence of our footprints as we trod the sacred paths of Francis, Clare and their followers.

Word, Images And Photography

Early September.
Warm sun shares the day
with cloud and showers.
In early afternoon,
pilgrims arrive wearily
at Casa Il Rosario,
a convent nestled in the heart of Rome.

Communicating through smiles and gestures,
the sisters show us to our rooms,
cells small and plain.
Some windows overlook city street
while others face an inner court.

By evening we are revived enough
to wander Roman roads.

The streets of Rome
sparkle wetly in morning sun.

St. Peter's Basilica is magnificent:
incredible mosaics, massive marble,
papal tombs, altars ornate,
Bernini's bronze canopy,
Michelangelo's Pieta.

Swiss guards colourfully
keep watch.
Clerics, monks and nuns in varied garb
mingle with gazing tourists
and praying pilgrims,
all one.

St. John Lateran,
ancient cathedral of saints and popes.

Here in 1209,
St. Francis of Assisi
received from Innocent III
approval of his Rule of Life.

Here today,
pilgrims still enter the presence of God.

Midst thunder and rain burst
the cloisters enchant.
Within the basilica
an essence of pilgrims
from centuries past.

On a door, these words:
*A pilgrimage is a path of conversion,
an interior preparation
for a renewal of the heart.*

The highway to Assisi
leaves the cobblestones of Rome
to wind through a countryside
of hills, vineyards and orchards.

The hills are dotted with structures
of stucco, brick and stone:
huts and houses,
churches and abbies,
castles in ruin.

Along the autostrada,
signs point to places
known to Francis:
Terni, Spolito,
Foligno, Perugia,
Assisi!

In Assisi
at St. Anthony's Guest House
we stay with Franciscan Sisters
of the Atonement.

Below my window,
tiered gardens drop downward
to St. Clare's Plaza.

A lizard peers from flowerpot
before venturing across
a pebbled path
to climb a tree.

God is near.

Church bells waken us to
grey skies, dampened streets,
towers and steeples veiled in mist.

After morning prayer,
we set out in gentle rain
to follow the determined steps
of Brother Alan.

We pray at San Rufino whose piazza
enclosed Clare's childhood home,
where Francis and Clare were both baptized,
where Clare received the palm branch
from the bishop.

We visit San Francesco Piccolino
where legend says Pica gave birth to Francis
and Chiesa Nuova where Francis lived.

At Santa Maria Maggiore
we behold ancient frescoes
once gazed upon
by the saints of Assisi.

We stand on the stones of Piazza Vescovado
where Francis rejected his birthright
to choose the nakedness of Christ.

Huddled beneath umbrellas
at a small street corner,
we stare at plain stone walls
awaiting Brother Alan's explanation
while our guide enjoys our suspense.

Finally he points out an unassuming building
once the Church of San Gregorio
where Francis felt called to be a knight.
Across the street is the former home
of the first brother to follow Francis,
Bernard of Quintavalle.
Two wonderful surprises!

At night prayer, we pilgrims share
insights, inspiration and gratitude
for our cheerful friar.

We go to bed to the distant sounds
of joyful singing and instrumental music
drifting through our open windows,
the annual Assisi Youth Festival.

Today a road trip by private coach
to Franciscan sites of the Rieti Valley:
Greccio, Fonte Columbo
and Poggio Bustone.

Through the bus window,
the exotic Italian countryside,
industrial buildings,
vineyards, olive orchards,
small farms, chickens, sheep,
ever-charming medieval hill top towns,
an ancient friary.

The houses, high and isolated,
plain and shuttered on the outside,
are two and three-storied
with lots of stairs.
Palm trees grow alongside pines.

On the Autostrada del Sol,
cars pass between trucks and buses
– even around curves –
using the centre line as third lane!

Initially startled, I soon realize
that in this country
such maneuvering is commonplace.

Arriving at Greccio in rain,
we climb wide stone steps
to enter the Christmas chapel.
Brother Alan relates the story
of the ivory bambino,
enthralling pilgrim strangers.

Crèches from around the world,
honouring this holy site where,
three years before his death,
Francis created a new Bethlehem.

Candles and torches lit up that long ago night
revealing manger, hay, ox and ass,
delighting men and beasts,
woods ringing with village voices,
the saint of God overcome with love,
a priest experiencing new consolation.

In the monastery built by Saint Bonaventure,
an ancient dormitory, the cell of Francis,
a portrait conveying simplicity, humility,
suffering:
an ailing Francis wiping his eye.

Before we depart, we eat bag lunches
and catch a glimpse of Francis' joy at creation,
the expanse of the Rieti valley.

At Fonte Columbo, fountain of doves,
Francis wrote his final Rule of Life in 1223.
O sacred cave and fountain spring
far below via a steep walk.

In the Chapel of the Magdelene,
where Francis painted his signature,
a Tau, we renew our commitment
to Franciscan life and reflect
on Gospel living.

So moving and poignant to revitalize
our promises in the very place
that the Franciscan Rule was born!
What joy and peace and hope!

So touching to then visit
the dormitory where Francis
endured cauterization
for his ailing eyes.

This is the Rule and Life
of the Friars Minor,
of the Order of Poor Clares,
and of the Brothers and Sisters
of the Third Order Regular:
to observe the holy Gospel
of our Lord Jesus Christ
by living in obedience,
without property, and in chastity.

The rule and life of Third Order
Secular Franciscans is this:
to observe the gospel of our Lord Jesus Christ
by following the example of Saint Francis of
Assisi,
who made Christ the inspiration and centre
of his life with God and people.

Secular Franciscans
should devote themselves especially
to careful reading of the gospel,
going from gospel to life
and life to gospel.

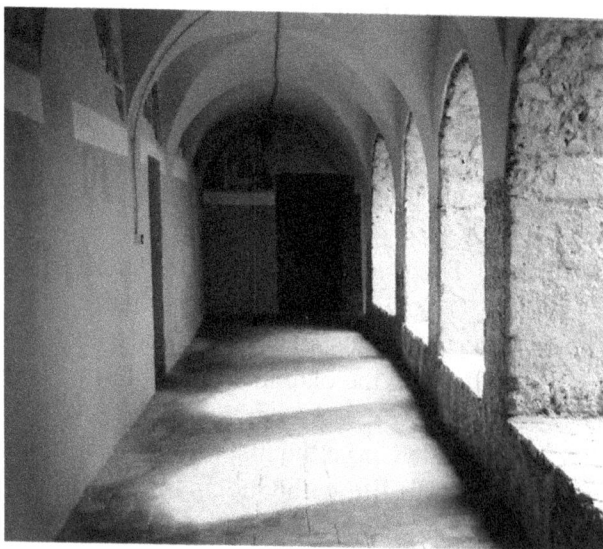

Early in his ministry,
Francis and six companions
came upon a deserted hermitage:
Poggio Bustone, high, rugged, impressive.

In ancient monastic tradition,
prayerful isolation is a principal support
of contemplative life.

From the monastery church of San Giancomo,
with the Rieti Valley exposed before us,
we are awed at the privilege
of being in this sacred place
of stark beauty.

Here in a cave, Francis confessed his faults
and asked to be shown his sins.
Here we reflect upon reconciliation,
Francis' and our own.
Here we give thanks for the gifts
of Francis and Clare
and for our fellow pilgrims.

Mount Subasio shelters caves and huts
where Francis and his friars prayed and dwelt.
One of these caves became a chapel
to which is attached a hermitage,
the Carceri.

In this secluded place, Francis appealed
to Sylvester and Clare to help him choose
between prayer and preaching.
They discerned that he should be
both mendicant and contemplative,
an itinerant preacher strengthened
with periods of solitary prayer.

In the cave of Francis,
a sister pilgrim experiences anguish,
envisioning her brother's imprisonment
and death in a Philippine cell.
But then, a stone from Carceri trails
pressed into her hand radiates warmly,
granting Franciscan peace.

I sit on a bench overlooking the valley
and photograph the sun
peeking through the forest canopy.
Birds sing and the wind blows gently.

The beauty of nature can bring God close
only to a certain point,
beyond that a distraction.

One must empty oneself completely
In order to experience God
in the depth of one's soul.

At the Carceri,
Brother Alan reflects that piety
is best suited for glorifying
and responding to God's glory.
Piety does not equal prayer.
Rooted deeper in our psyche and soul,
prayer is the prima facie viaduct
through which God speaks to us.

To pray well, we must bring ourselves
to a place of silence where we become
transformed into the likeness
of Francis, Clare and Jesus.
Then we are at the beginnings
of becoming prayer.

The friar finds his cave
across the ravine at the end of the trail,
the place where he had begun his friendship
with silence and contemplation.

Though many visitors have been here since,
leaving crosses, prayer, postcards
in the niches of the walls,
he finds his own card, the writing still visible.
This place is sacred to Bro. Alan Gaebel,
OFM Cap July 20, 1999.

Although Clare's body
lies in the crypt at Santa Chiara,
it is at San Damiano that I feel
the presence of the saint.

We wander through Clare's dormitory,
chapel and cloister,
awed by the simplicity
and sacredness of the place.

Francis loved San Damiano,
having rebuilt the church himself.
Giving it to Clare and her sisters
was a gift from his heart.

At Santa Chiara,
we visit the tomb of Clare,
and kneel before the image
of the crucified Saviour
where Francis devoutly prayed.
Francis, do you not see that my house
falls into ruin?
Go, and repair it for me.

Many came to live with Clare at San Damiano:
first Agnes, her sister, and Pacifica di
Guelfuccio,
companion that Palm Sunday night
as they fled to the Portiuncula.

Soon other girls, noble, rich, young and pretty,
could not resist the call of San Damiano.
Happy to give their dowries to the poor,
they went barefoot, cut their hair,
enclosed in the little convent.

There, in strictest poverty,
they discovered the happiness
vainly sought at banquets,
a peace not found in the world.

When Francis wished that Clare
be abbess, she resisted for three years
before becoming, at age twenty-one,
servant of the sisters,
considering it privilege
to work the hardest
and eat the least.

At Saint Clare's Basilica I pray
before the gaze of the Jesus
that spoke to Francis.

Longing for a keepsake
of the crucifix which once had hung
in the little church of San Damiano,
I furtively snap two photos
which, when later developed
are somewhat faded,
pale like my own spiritual vision.

A small display In Saint Clare's crypt,
contains the Papal Bull granting her
the privilege of Poverty as she lay dying.

Gentle Clare, faithful servant of God,
defender of women's rights,
loyal to the Church.

Early morning Assisi.

Beyond the nearby
Church of Santa Chiara,
everything is veiled in mist,
the sky above blue
with wispy streaks of white.

Soft music floats through
guesthouse foyer and halls.
Today at breakfast,
the instrumental music
from Madame Butterfly.

In chapel, a Reading from James:
be merciful, not judgmental;
if your faith does not have works,
what good is it?

More a trickle than a river,
Rivo Torto presumably held more water
in the time of Francis.

Here Francis and his companions
first settled after the Pope approved their Rule.
Here the brothers lived in wattle huts
and cared for lepers, seeing Jesus
in these rejected ones.

Below the city of peace,
we visit the Assisi War Cemetery
honouring soldiers who died in World War II.
We wander solemnly among tombstones
marked with names and ages of the dead,
young men in their prime.

In the Canadian section,
where flowers grace every grave,
we pilgrims are truly moved.

Brother Alan has arranged
for our privileged eyes
to see Santa Maria della Spina,
now privately owned.
The rough little leper church,
built by Francis and his brothers,
is beautiful in its simplicity.

St. Mary of the Angels
shelters the tiny Portiuncula,
cradle of Franciscan spirituality,
inside its magnificent walls.

After a Benedictine abbot
gave the Portiuncula to Francis,
the brothers gratefully
encircled the poor little church
with their humble huts.

Although the abbot and his monks
demanded no payment or rent,
Francis annually sent
a basket of small fish to the monks
who in return offered the gift
of a vessel of oil.

I touch the stone with my hands,
sensing the holy hands of Francis upon it.
The crowds here today make it difficult
to be alone with Francis.

I remind myself that in my busy world
it seems challenging to be alone with Jesus.
But Jesus is always there…
waiting for me.

Under overcast skies
we Franciscans set out for Tuscany
through hilly Italian countryside:
thirteen seculars, two Capuchins,
a Sister of Atonement and two Sisters
of Mary Immaculate.

A winding climbing road leads to Cortona,
its ancient buildings close to the road.
Large, hard rain drops
splatter against the bus.

All is grey, gloomy and wet
when we arrive at a grey stone church
in a stark, bare setting.

Here lies the body
of Margaret of Cortona,
first Third Order Secular saint,
lying perpetually in state
before the altar of her church.

We reach La Celle
as the sun bursts through.
Summoned by bell, Brother Pietro
conducts our private tour.
In awe we move through chambers
of ancient stone and wood,
admiring the refectory built by Brother Elias,
the choir's expressively carved crucifix,
the chapel's simplicity, the grille designed
for viewing the consecration during Mass.

Winding asphalt carries us
across the Appenine Mountains,
through wooded mountainous regions,
past little stone shrines in remote places,
and tiny huts with oval, open doorways
to beautiful Monte Cassale.

Beneath a grape arbour, we enjoy
bagged lunches prepared by the guesthouse.
Then friars welcome us with cappuccino
before guiding us through the sacred,
charming, ancient hermitage.

I steal back to the cell of St. Anthony,
patron of my home fraternity,
with mischievous Teodora
who obligingly takes my picture there.
Outside again, we wander by terraced gardens
and enclosures of chickens and goats.

In their isolation and simplicity, the hermitages
are physically and spiritually magnificent.
How blessed and grateful we are
to experience these holy Franciscan sites!

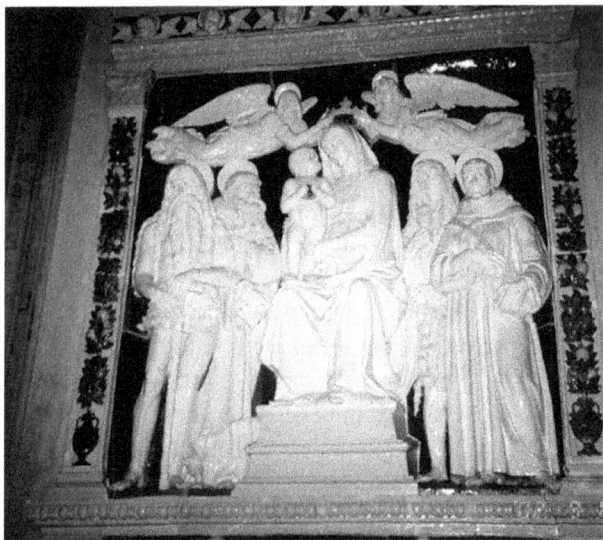

As we head for the holy mountain,
skies cloud over, showers resume.
La Verna, drenched with rain,
is huge, bleak, stark and sprawling.

Noisy hordes of tourists and
orange plastic fencing assail our senses.
Workmen, quiet and patient,
ignore pilgrim and tourist
to repair masonry and shovel earth.

Rain-soaked, we visit the cave of the
Projecting Rock, the magnificent della Robbias,
the Chapel of the Stigmata, the cells
of Francis, Bonaventure and Anthony.

Jim finds a secret entrance to ancient cloisters!
I follow through an unmarked chapel door,
down cavernous halls, immense and bare,
to the old cloister, library, St. Clare's hall.

But inexplicably, I feel as empty
as the shrine's interior corridors,
unable to rekindle the earlier joy
experienced at the hermitages.

Riding back to Assisi,
the pilgrims admit to dejection,
spirits as dampened as the stone buildings
and puddled streets we pass.

Then in the sky a rainbow:
sign of God's covenant!

Early this morning our lizard
walks casually across the lower terrace
while Bach plays quietly in the guesthouse.
When music shifts to Celtic strains,
a piper plays a slow, plaintive 'Danny Boy',
bringing tears to my eyes because today,
September 11, is the first anniversary
of attacks on the New York towers
and the Pentagon.

In the lower and upper churches
of the Basilica of San Francesco,
we gaze upon ancient frescoes
of Giotto, Cimabue and Lorenzetti.
At the tomb of Francis, I present petitions
from my Fraternity and of my heart.
How blessed to be in this holy place.

Through Brother Alan's influence,
we gain admission to the Sacro Convento.
In delighted silence, we walk old corridors,
pass cloisters, and attend mass in the Peace Chapel,
our Eucharist coinciding in American time
with the original acts of terrorism.

In late afternoon,
I hang laundry in the lower garden,
the simple task a prayer in such peace and beauty.
During Night Prayer, we celebrate the Transitus.
Brother Alan has arranged seven candles
in the form of a cross.

In flickering light, we share the day's experiences,
speak of conversion and vocation,
and thank our friar for his loving attentiveness
to our endless needs.

Our last full day in Assisi is a 'Free Day'.
We pilgrims hardly know what to do or see.
Every minute, every second is so precious.

After Morning Prayer, we wander the little city
saying good-bye in our hearts to the sacred
stones
of the ancient streets and buildings.

There's a spiritual magnetism in this holy place,
the earth itself exuding energy, wisdom, history,
the essence of Francis, Clare and their
companions!

Jim and I take a final stroll of the
lovely gardens of St. Anthony's Guest House.
Damaged in the earthquake, the guesthouse,
like much of Assisi, has been lovingly restored.

After lunch at Tavola Calda Dal Karro,
we buy cheese and meat for evening munching.
As we return to the guesthouse, I take a final
picture
of a group of Mother Teresa's Sisters of Mercy
in front of Chiesa Nuova.

On behalf of us all, Margaret has bought a gift
for Brother Alan to show our appreciation
of his planning, devotion and care.

Oh! How I hate to say good-bye!

As we take leave of the guesthouse for Rome,
a nun gives us each a prayer card with their
Patronal Prayer to Our Lady of the Atonement
and other guardian saints.

En route to Casa Il Rosario, I converse with
Beatrice.
Beneath her unassuming quietness,
she is a woman of faith and courage
who has endured many trials and challenges.
How little we know of our creature earthlings,
each with heart, soul and story.

Jim and I spend time at St. Peter's Basilica in
prayer,
and in the evening, we walk through Rome.
The back streets of Rome have many secrets:
lovely courtyards hidden within plain alleys,
pleasant inner laneways glimpsed through
gateways,
elegant apartments concealed behind austere
walls.

On our way back to Il Rosario,
we pass an open courtyard where, on a wall,
a movie is projected for people seated casually
on benches and a central fountain.

Preparing for bed, I reluctantly acknowledge
that we are now in rapid transition
from pilgrim to tourist.

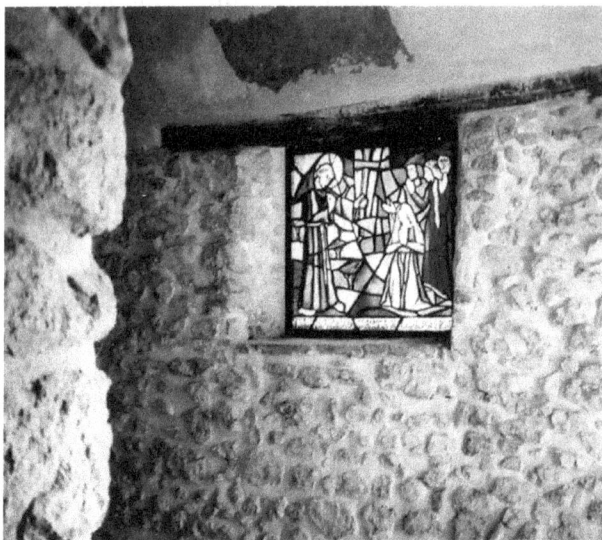

At dawn, I lie awake listening to the sound of nuns at
prayer,
their chants and song drifting through the building.
In the distance, church bells ring while, below our
window,
the alley echoes with laughter and occasional shouts.
Motor scooters roar between cars,
and garbage trucks clank and bang.
A dog barks.

Then singing and chanting floats across the lane,
probably from another convent.
Rome is the epitome of contrasts!

After breakfast, we stop in churches,
including the Church of Maria above the Medina.
We admire the Pantheon's granite columns and
massive dome,
visit the baroque Trevi Fountain, and linger on the
Spanish Steps.
We enter the Hassler Hotel where we are courteously
told that
'for security reasons' we cannot leave the lobby.

On this last night in Rome, I seek a parting sign.
Drawn by chanting and singing from across the way,
I lean out my window and read "Residence S. Pietro"
on a stone address block a few doors down.
Prayers float heavenward from its windows,
as they do from Il Rosario, blending beautifully
with the sounds of everyday life.

Exultation fills my soul,
discernment of the sought-for sign,
a vision of spirit-filled communities dotting the earth,
gracing all of creation.

Pilgrimage has been described as
exterior mysticism
while mysticism is considered
internal pilgrimage.

Living and praying in and near Assisi
blesses one with vivid impressions
of places inhabited by the
brothers and sisters of Francis.

We pray for grace to include
elements of internal pilgrimage
in our continuing travels.

St. Francis was in the world
but not of it,
St. Clare, apart but involved,
the Gospel their guide,
the model for our journeying.

Like the saints of Assisi
we pilgrims strive
to balance prayer and solitude
with service to others.

BOOK II
Forth From the Garden

Therefore the LORD GOD sent him
forth from the garden of Eden,
to till the ground from which he was taken.
And at the east of the garden of Eden
he placed the cherubim,
and a sword flaming and turning
to guard the way to the tree of life.
Genesis 3:23

Introduction

What is it about the spirituality of Saints Francis and Clare that calls to our yearning souls? Twenty-five years ago during a period of personal darkness, I myself was drawn to the secular branch of Third Order Franciscans. Seeking spiritual growth and inner peace, in due course I found both.

It began with a notice in our church bulletin announcing an information night on the Third Order of St. Francis for interested persons in the area. For several years preceding this fortuitous announcement, I had been inquiring about the Third Order while making annual retreats at a Capuchin centre in Michigan. Delighted about the possibility of a local Franciscan presence, I attended the information night. Approximately sixty of us gathered for the occasion.

I have to admit that I found the large number unsettling since small, intimate groups are more in keeping with my reserved nature. But I would soon find that my concern was naïve. The secular branch of Franciscanism is an authentic Order in the Catholic Church, not a prayer group or service club. To become professed in this Order, one must first undergo a period of formation and discernment. Following the Rule of Francis is a lifestyle, a vocation. Thus, only a few of the attendees would feel called to serve Jesus as Secular Franciscans.

Eight were received into the Order after three months of prayer and study. Six of us would be professed more than a year later. A Seminarian serving his pastoral year in the parish joined us for much of our formative journey. Two of the original eight candidates died during the period between reception and profession.

Along the way, we learned that there are three main branches in the Franciscan family. The First Order founded by Francis is comprised of Friars Minor. The Second Order, known as the Poor Clares, follows the Rule of Clare of Assisi. The Third Order consists of religious brothers and sisters as well as secular members. To distinguish Third Order lay members from those taking religious vows, the Vatican II Council decreed that the former should be called Secular Franciscans.

We learned too that, unlike earlier monastic traditions that built upon the lifestyle of the first Christian communities described in the Acts of the Apostles, Francis sought to actively live the Gospel. He desired to live as Jesus and his disciples lived when they walked upon the earth.

Francis taught his followers to immerse themselves in Gospel living, going from Gospel to life and life to Gospel, trusting in the mercy of God and the enlightenment of the Holy Spirit.

The Gospel life of Francis is one of ongoing repentance and conversion sustained by faith in a loving, forgiving God. It is confidence in the power of continuous conversion that gives Franciscans their inner peace. It is awareness of Francis' appreciation for the beauty of Creation that enhances communal joy.

We also learned that our Fraternity was not a new one, but the restoration of one that had been dormant for twenty-five years. Some elderly members of the original Fraternity still resided in the area, following the Rule privately.

And now another twenty-five years have passed. During this time, new brothers and sisters have joined us while others have died or moved away. There are usually around twenty of us, the numbers swelling or ebbing as do the tides of creation. So much can happen in a quarter century.

The history of our Fraternity is recorded in its Minutes, but the prayerful, courageous lives of individual members have not been documented. Those who have already departed have taken their testimonies with them. When I asked Fraternity members to consider giving witness to the mysterious peace of Jesus that rules their lives, they prayed on the matter. As I had hoped, several agreed to share their stories.

In listening to personal, often painful details from their pasts, I was tremendously moved by the trust they placed in me. As they reminisced, wispy memories from the secret archives of the heart occasionally surfaced to be prayed over and recommitted to the everlasting righteousness of God.

Several related that they had never told their stories before. Moved and sometimes surprised by things remembered, they found it therapeutic to ponder experiences from their pasts. Many welcomed the opportunity to leave a brief history for their children and grandchildren. All hoped that they might motivate, inspire or reassure others.

These poignant accounts of faith, commitment, joy, anguish and perseverance could be a collection of short stories, but they are not fiction. They are love stories celebrating the graces alive in souls thirsting for God. Common threads running through these stories are prayerfulness, forgiveness, patience, service and thanksgiving. You will meet heroic individuals who overcame childhoods of neglect to become motivating role models. Others currently endure loneliness, misunderstanding or illness with courage, acceptance and trust in God.

There is the missionary couple who ended up remaining in a city they were just passing through. There is a woman who wanted to be a nun but was called to minister to people outside the convent.

People who persevered through difficulties in their marriages, yet were rewarded with fulfilment in later years, provide encouragement to those walking that same path now. Women who raised children alone while their husbands were absent through work, attitude or design recognize in hindsight the unmistakable guiding hand of God. There are accounts of social activists who helped bring justice to a world mired in materialism and apathy, and of individuals searching for spiritual focus and depth.

You will be touched by the stories of a man whose entire family was erased through illness and massacre while he was still a young boy, and of a woman courageously reconciled to the bewildering progress of Alzheimer's. Persons grieving for loved ones lost through death or circumstance speak to the hearts of all.

Ever since Adam and Eve disobeyed God and were expelled from Eden, we have struggled with our weakened natures as well as with disappointments and the failings of our companions. As described in Genesis 3:23, *sent forth from the garden* by the LORD GOD, we are compelled to *till the ground* until we regain paradise.

Midst trial and tribulation, the men and women whose stories are documented in the following pages found peace in the Rule of the Secular Franciscan Order. They relate their stories with the tranquility and hope governing souls aware that they are embraced by God. They were gifted with graces distributed outside Eden's gates.

St. Francis founded his Third Order in 1209, the same year in which he established the First Order. At the time, he promised a Rule* for those who became his disciples while continuing to live in the world and in their homes. The first Rule directed the Brothers and Sisters of Penance, as he called them, to observe God's commandments and to live the Gospel as closely as it was possible for persons living secular lives world.

While striving after the Gospel life, we have travelled a complex journey straddling heaven and earth. Sometimes it seems that the years have flown. Other times it's as if we've been trudging along forever. Whatever our frame of mind, we know that this is merely a short span on the road to eternity.

The names of individuals in the following chapters have been changed at their request.

---

* It is commonly believed that the *Letter to the Brothers and Sisters of Penance* may have been that first rule. *A formal Rule was given to them by the Church in 1221, after fraternities of the Third Order had been established in various cities. This Rule was revised in 1289, and again in 1883. The new Rule was approved by Pope Paul VI in 1978.*

Omnibus of Sources, page 1941

I

AGNES

Agnes is a welcoming lady who dresses tastefully. She lives in a pleasant apartment overlooking Lake Huron with her twelve-year-old cat, her companion since her husband's death. She became a Secular Franciscan in 1985 and was professed in the Order in 1987. She finds Francis amazing, she says, and feels akin to him in his love for nature, gardening, and animals. For years, she has kept a statue of St. Francis in her garden as well as in her home. In her typically generous way, she donated one of her beautiful Francis statues to our Fraternity where it retains a place of honour at all our gatherings.

Agnes was born in Regina and lived there until age thirteen. Alcoholism runs in her family. Her father was a bank manager who moved around a lot. He drank whenever he came home from work. Her mother had "a glass of Old Vienna in her hand all day". Weekends were hell, she states.

Agnes relates two early childhood memories. When she was six, her mother took her for a ride in their new car, a "Marmon". A woman friend was sitting in the back, and Agnes sat in the front beside her mother. She regained consciousness to find herself in a field leaning against a barbed wire fence. All three had been thrown from the car which then lay upside down, its engine roaring and wheels spinning. "Only by God's grace am I here," reflects Agnes. On another occasion, she recalls sitting in the back seat of a car driven by her father. She was holding a doll wrapped in a beautiful satin cover. When the car became stuck, her father used the doll's satin cover for traction to get the car out. He told his daughter that he would replace it, but he never did.

High school years were similarly difficult. When Agnes was a teenager living in Toronto, she had a close girlfriend. One day, the friend and her parents came to dinner by invitation from Agnes' mother. When the guests arrived, her mother was on the front porch waiting to welcome them - in her housecoat. After that, the friend would have nothing to do with her. Remorseful, Agnes' mother dressed up and went to visit the friend's mother. Unfortunately, her efforts did not rekindle the lost friendship between the girls.

Her mother died at the age of fifty-three from a bathroom fall. Later, her father married a woman who made him stop drinking. Agnes has an older brother whose two wives left him because of his binge drinking. Over time, Agnes lost touch with him and, when their father died, she had to contact him through the police. Repulsed by the alcoholism that had so affected her life, she continued to avoid her brother for many more years. She avoided alcohol until age forty but now permits herself a social glass of wine.

Following her husband's death, Agnes felt guilty about not seeing her only sibling. Being a Franciscan by that time, she had the grace and inner strength to seek reconciliation with him. Assisted by her daughter, she located her brother in a Toronto seniors' home. After several telephone conversations, she invited him to visit. The elderly man came by train, grateful for the reunion. Now ill, moderation has been forced upon him: he is allowed only a little wine by his caregivers.

When Agnes finished high school, she wanted to go to Business College, but her mother suggested she enlist in the air force as a secretary. She received a subsistence allowance from the military while taking a course in Toronto. After basic training in Rockcliff on the outskirts of Ottawa, she returned to Toronto for a further month of training and military drill.

She was posted as a secretary in the training administration department at Mountainview near Belleville. There she met an intellectual young flight sergeant who would become her husband. Born in England, he had come to Canada with his mother and sister after his father died in World War I. His mother remarried and the family moved to Sarnia. In 1939, he enlisted to serve in the second Great War.

At Mountainview, the young sergeant brought Agnes a gift from the men in appreciation for her office work. Agnes was flattered and impressed to learn that he had been on his high school debating team. She especially liked that he didn't drink. Early on, he wanted to be a minister although Agnes feels that his expectations of parishioners would have been too high. Because her husband-to-be was being posted to England, they were married in 1944, less than a year after they'd met. Initially, a priest refused to marry them since it would be a mixed marriage. Agnes' mother came to the rescue, phoned a monsignor who interviewed the young man and arranged for instructions by the Mountainview chaplain. Agnes notes that her husband died fifty-three years plus a day after their February 11, 1944 wedding.

After she was discharged from the Air Force, Agnes worked in a photography studio in Belleville. Her husband, discharged six months later as the war was winding down, accepted a job at Polymer in Sarnia. They moved there and within five years had three children, two daughters and a son. Her husband built a stucco house on a triple lot in the country. The family moved back to the city when the children were older. The children attended Catholic schools and, on Sundays, accompanied their mother to church.

The first ten years of their marriage were "not too pleasant", Agnes says. Her husband could be demanding and domineering, and being eight years older as well as male, expected to be in charge. He begrudged Agnes going to the movies once a month with a female friend, complaining that the friend was a bad influence. He was also an exacting father. One Christmas he persuaded their younger daughter to give away her beautiful new doll, and accompanied her on their 'charitable' mission.

In time, he acknowledged that his authoritarian nature was making his wife unhappy. He promised to turn over a new leaf, and did in fact, make an effort. The couple had their fourth child when Agnes was forty-one and planning to study nursing. Although the pregnancy changed her career plans and she had a difficult pregnancy, Agnes acknowledges that their new daughter's arrival was good for her and her husband, keeping them both young. When it came to painting, wallpapering or laying floors, Agnes and her husband were a good team. He figured out the details while she did the fussy work. Having an artistic flair, she was also an expert seamstress and enjoyed oil painting.

Before she became a Secular Franciscan, Agnes was active in Cursillo for many years. Cursillo made her want to expand her spiritual horizons. She was on several teams and gave three talks. Since it's customary for men to go on Cursillo weekends before their wives, Agnes' husband accommodatingly attended the weekend program so that Agnes could participate. Although he "came home flying" from the weekend, he did not continue with Cursillo. Agnes is grateful that he went that one time for her.

Having promised God that she would stick with her marriage, Agnes moved with her husband to a lakeside home where they lived for thirty more years. An introvert and not terribly social, her husband spent hours at his computer. Agnes is happy to relate that he mellowed as he aged, allowing the couple to enjoy a pleasant relationship. Although Agnes and her husband had little alcohol in their home, two of their children developed drinking problems. One has overcome it. Agnes' three older children are married and live in the area allowing her to enjoy many of her nine grandchildren and three great grandchildren at close range. At the time of this interview, she was looking forward to a forthcoming trip to Vancouver for her grandson's wedding. Her youngest daughter works at a law firm in Toronto.

Secular Franciscans are expected to have an apostolate, an area of service in the name of Jesus. This is hardly a challenge for Agnes. Observing her skills at decorating the altar for each service and Liturgical Season, the pastor made her 'environment coordinator'. At the opening ceremony of the new church, wearing a white dress and gold accessories, she bowed to the bishop, wiped down the altar with oil, and with a friend's assistance, brought out the altar cloth. She continued decorating the altar for eight years.

She has been actively involved in her parish as a Eucharistic Minister and Reader and still brings Communion to a parishioner on her way home from Sunday Mass. She belongs to the Caring and Sharing ministry, visiting residents at a nursing home. Four times a week, she feeds lunch to a woman with multiple sclerosis. She speaks admiringly of this "marvelous lady who is so smart and always cheerful".

For the past ten years, Agnes has courageously endured a condition which affects her speech. Spasmodic dysphonia affects the same part of the brain as Parkinson's does. In order to have audible speech, she must travel by train to Toronto every three months for Botox injections into her larynx.

True to her spirit, Agnes insists that she is grateful for her good health, independence, and the fact that she can still drive. Ever empathetic to others, she enjoys the story of Francis' sensitivity to the friar suffering midnight hunger pangs.[1]

II

JOSEPH AND THERESA

Still grieving the recent death of their youngest son, Joseph and Theresa hide their sadness behind stoic smiles. Secular Franciscans since 1997, they are both cherished by our Fraternity.

Born in Slovakia, Joseph was the third of five children, two sisters and three brothers. Tragically, most of the family died young, his father and a sister of typhus. By the time Joseph was eight years old, only he and a two-year-old brother remained of the family. Joseph went to live with his gentle and loving grandparents. His young brother was taken in by a childless aunt and uncle who doted on him.

But death continued to pursue the family. Early one morning two years later, while Joseph attended church with his grandmother, guerrillas entered the home of his aunt and uncle, and murdered both of them as well as Joseph's little brother.

As a youth, Joseph went to the city to apprentice in radio technology. At the age of nineteen he began the required two years of army service. Returning to his own village, he worked at a radio transmitter station for ten years. The next five years were spent at a television station in Bratislava.

Theresa was raised on a Slovakian farm with two brothers and a sister. Their father was not religious, but their mother, who came from a closely-knit family, made everyone attend Sunday Mass as well as to vespers on May and October evenings. As teenagers, the children were never excused from Sunday Mass even if they had been out dancing late on Saturday nights.

Joseph met Theresa through a cousin when she was sixteen and he was seven years older. They dated for two years and broke after Theresa heard of his other girlfriends. Ten months later they bumped into each other at a dance and resumed their romance. They married six months later. At the time, Joseph was working at a radio station and Theresa was working as an office bookkeeper. Their first son was born a year later. Theresa continued to work between babies, but stopped working after the birth of a third son. The family moved from their small village to Bratislava where Joseph was employed at a television station. In his off-hours, Joseph, who had acquired skills at carpentry, electricity and plumbing, built a house for his family in each location.

When the Russian occupation took place in 1968 on August 21, the people of Slovakia feared the worst. Joseph was especially anxious. During his time in the army, he had been a candidate in the communist party but postponed signing on to the party for three years before finally saying 'No'. When communist officials demanded an explanation, he gave the excuse that his grandparents wouldn't approve. After the Russian takeover, he was afraid that, because of this past refusal, he might be punished.

By happy chance, the family had just acquired passports and were able to get visas for a 'three-day holiday to Austria'. They left at once, leaving behind a new car and their house, and giving the house key to an aunt. In hindsight, Joseph believes that the government wanted rid of perceived rebels because 100,000 people were readily permitted to depart Slovakia at the time.

In Austria they stayed at a monastery with friends for three days. Then they went to Switzerland for four months while Joseph worked for an electrician. Back in Slovakia, Theresa's father sold their house and sent them the money.

The family came to Canada in late December when friends told them Sarnia was a good place to live. Their sons were aged three, four and seven. Theresa worked at a donut shop, taking the night shift because of her poor English. Finding it difficult to care for her young family, she threatened to quit after three months and was given the day shift. Joseph worked for a television and appliance business and joined the labour union. Soon he also joined the carpenters union and began working for a construction company. As a sideline, he built houses, using the multi-skills he had acquired in Slovakia.

Thriftily, the family moved into older homes which they fixed up and sold for a profit before moving on to the next house. They went to the Slovak church every Sunday with their children, enjoying the company of the Slovakian community. Theresa missed her family, especially at Christmas but was unable to visit because their homeland was now part of communist Czechoslovakia. Finally after ten years, she travelled to Poland where her mother's sister lived. Her family came to visit her there. By this time, her siblings had children of their own, and Theresa's mother talked enthusiastically about these grandchildren.

Feeling out of touch with her old country family, Theresa came to the unexpected realization that she was more comfortable in her Canadian environment. She returned to her husband in Canada, permanently cured of her homesickness.

Ten years later Theresa was able to visit Czechoslovakia. In order to do so, however, she was required to fill out special papers, ask for forgiveness, and pay for the education she had received in Slovakia. She was then free to spend five weeks with her sister and mother and to attend the wedding of her brother's son. Theresa's prayerful mother arranged for a month of Masses for her Canadian daughter's family. But Theresa, not overly religious at the time, took the gift lightly. As the visit drew to a close, Theresa's sister suffered a ruptured brain aneurism. She died at the age of forty-nine, shortly after Theresa's return to Canada.

In 1992 Joseph and Theresa travelled to Czechoslovakia together. They returned to find that their middle son's wife had left with the couple's baby. Concerned for the infant's welfare, Joseph and Theresa were able to obtain custody of the child until she attained the age of twelve.

Theresa felt drawn to increased prayer and in 1994 was consecrated to the Blessed Mother as was Joseph a year later. They began to meet other faith-filled people, and Joseph said that, strengthened by devotion to Mary, he experienced a dramatic change in his life. He had a vision of Mary on May 31 and the resultant joy carried him along for five or six years. Two years after their consecration to the Blessed Mother, Theresa and Joseph went to Medugorje. So motivated were they by the pilgrimage that they fasted every Wednesday and Friday for the following year.

Sometime afterward, someone told Theresa that if she asked her guardian angel what his name was, the angel would reveal it in a dream. Theresa asked her angel for this grace, but when she awoke the following morning, she found herself saying aloud, "Francis of Assisi... Francis of Assisi... Francis of

Assisi." Disappointed at not learning the angel's name, she dismissed the incident.

Shortly afterwards, she read a notice in the Petrolia church bulletin inviting persons seeking deeper spirituality to explore the Secular Franciscan Order. Theresa recalled the experience of reciting the name of the saint of Assisi and reflected on the fact that her mother had died in 1995 on St. Francis' Feast Day, October 4. Additionally, in the year of her mother's death, Theresa had been on pilgrimage in Quebec with a Secular Franciscan whose holiness she admired. And so, inspired by these divine proddings, Theresa and Joseph decided to attend the Franciscan information night.

Soon thereafter they began the Formation process. The welcoming attitude of the formation team and the loving support of the fraternity became an important part of their lives. In 1999 Joseph and Theresa were professed in the Order. Initially they thought it would not be easy to follow the way of St. Francis, especially in becoming less materialistic. Theresa feels that she had to make more changes than Joseph. But being a Secular Franciscan is wonderful, they say. Francis teaches them how to bring simplicity into our modern lives. Joseph especially relates to the Saint's affinity to nature.

Joseph and Theresa are truly prayerful people. They love reciting the Office together. They pray the rosary daily, attend Mass most days and have been committed to a weekly hour at exposition of the

Blessed Sacrament for seven years. Every day they appeal to their guardian angels to protect them, their children and grandchildren. They pray the Angelus three times over the course of a day. Like many of our generation, they are concerned over their children's lack of church involvement. Theresa states that the Blessed Mother said that if only one person in a family prays for the children, those children will be saved. It's that promise that gives her hope and courage.

Their prayer life spills over into their daily lives. They are cheerful, welcoming, considerate, compassionate and genuinely affectionate. Joseph is a sacristan at church, and Theresa does pastoral visiting at a nursing home, bringing Holy Communion to the residents.

When their youngest son died on October 9, 2006, their spiritual grit was greatly tested. He was their "gentle son" who loved his brothers and their children. He was especially good to his parents, calling almost every day, taking his mom out for lunch on her birthday. Previously abandoned by his wife, he seemed to have recovered from his broken heart and was getting his life back on track. Now it was Joseph and Theresa whose hearts were broken.

Theresa and Joseph were moved that so many people loved him and came to the wake and funeral to share their grief. Their son's friends from work spoke of his sense of humour and his enjoyment of hockey and golf. The priest's homily was beautiful.

Slovak people did traditional Slovak singing at the gravesite. Of course, their Franciscan family was present throughout. It is when we lose someone we love that we most clearly see the worthlessness of material things, Theresa notes.

Instead of withdrawing into their pain, Joseph and Theresa courageously shared their experience of loss. Our spiritual lives are different when grief is fresh, they say. It's harder to pray when you're unhappy. Faith can remain strong but one's spirit is not the same. Like the Psalmist, they cry out to God, asking him why they are being punished, why he has turned away, why striving for holiness cannot prevent pain. They try to make sense of suffering. Sadness returns at unpredictable times. Is it because it's summer and their son loved summer so much?

Still, life goes on and others need them. Prayer gives them strength. Community supports them. One day at a time, they say.

Both are intrigued by the story of Francis handing over his clothes to the Bishop.[2] Joseph wonders how Francis could so abruptly return his clothes to his father, Pietro. He feels empathy for the father's hurt and anger. After all, Francis had been rather generous at his father's expense. Theresa, on the other hand, notes that she has always loved to give things away even when it didn't belong to her. As a child, she happily gave liquor and flowers to visitors, unaware that she was not entitled to give away her parents' belongings. Perhaps St. Francis had this same naïve generosity.

III

LIZ

In the many years that I have known Liz, she has been unfailingly gracious, gentle, compassionate and friendly. And like most, if not all of us, she has carried secret suffering within her serene presence. She is one of our original members who joined the newly-restored St. Anthony of Padua Fraternity twenty-five years ago. Her call to Franciscanism came during a period of personal distress. Seeking a spirituality that would provide her soul with nourishment and tranquility, the Rule of St. Francis has provided a sustaining foundation to her life.

Liz grew up in County Roscommon, Ireland, as a middle child in a family of ten children, two boys and eight girls. It was a beautiful part of the country with rolling hills and the River Shannon sparkling in the distance. Her father was a businessman who, by the time Liz was born, had bought a farm and moved his family there. He did not have a real knack for farming and the family worked hard to keep things going. Liz remembers her father as a strict, decent man who did his own thing and always dressed as a businessman rather than a farmer. Petrol was rationed and the family was pretty well on its own much of the time. The children's lives consisted mostly of farm work and homework.

Liz's mother was very prayerful. Liz remembers her singing, *Daily, Daily Sing to Mary.* A picture of Mary was prominent in the house and there was a small shrine known as the Sacred Heart Lamp. The Sacred Heart Lamp consisted of a red light burning at all times before a picture of the Sacred Heart inscribed with the names of all the children. On Sundays, her mother read the Lives of the Saints to her offspring. The family recited the rosary every night and walked to Sunday Mass in all kinds of weather.

A year before Liz completed high school, her father died from a stroke. In those days, young people were considered adults once they reached their teens. Since there was no work in Ireland, Liz arranged to train for a nurse in England. Before she was able to leave, her mother became seriously ill with colon cancer. When Liz visited her mother in hospital, a surgeon bluntly told her that that they had "just opened her up and closed her. We couldn't do a thing."

Liz was devastated. She recalls walking from the hospital wondering how it was possible for the world to continue on so normally. A month after she began her training, she received news of her mother's death. Her youngest sister was only two at the time. Coming home on the train from England, Liz heard about a "big funeral at the cemetery on the previous day." They were talking about her mother's funeral.

After three years of training in London, the young nurse returned to Ireland where she studied midwifery at the National Maternity Hospital in Dublin. It was so heavenly to be in Ireland that she thought she could never leave it again, and she was delighted when the matron at the Rotunda hired her.

Then she saw a notice that they were looking for nurses in Newfoundland, and on a whim, went for an interview. Soon Liz and another young nurse found themselves on a paid first class flight to Newfoundland. Despite engine trouble on the way across the Atlantic Ocean, they arrived safely at Gander. The place had been an army base, and the young women couldn't believe that people were living in wooden houses - dark green ones at that.

But their adventure was just beginning. A taxi drove them fifty miles over a gravel road through a dense evergreen forest to Lewis Port. There they boarded a motor boat which chugged out into the waves and rocks of the Atlantic to Twillingate. Liz thought that she would never see civilization again.

The only pastime at her new posting was walking

around the island. There was no Catholic church, and in winter, no boat crossing or mail delivery. She was invited to dinner on Christmas Day, but refused, believing it to be an intrusion on the family. In Ireland, nobody leaves their house on Christmas Day.

Although they had a two-year contract, the young women decided to leave after five months. The Ministry of Health arranged for one nurse to go to St Johns and the other to Grand Falls. Liz went to St. Johns.

There, an Irish nurse introduced her to a young physician who had come over from Ireland a couple of months earlier. He was handsome, charming, had attended private schools, was well-educated, fluent in Latin and extremely intelligent.

Although she was tremendously quiet and shy, they began dating. Sharing a common homeland, they both had played field hockey and both spoke Irish. Unlike Liz's family who also spoke English, the doctor's family spoke only Irish at home. The young doctor and nurse worked in the sanatorium until they married a year and a half later. In true Newfoundland style, the sanatorium put on the wedding reception for the couple.

They moved to Gander where their first daughter and son were born. Her husband then applied for radiology at McGill University Hospital, and a second son was born in Montreal. Two years later, in 1960, the family moved to Sarnia where the young physician was hired as radiologist. Four more children soon arrived, a daughter and three sons.

The family also took in a seven-year-old foster child because there was a shortage of Catholic foster homes. The boy had already been in twelve homes because of his problem behaviours. He continued to cause considerable trouble at school and in the community. While undergoing treatment at a residential facility, he came home for a Christmas visit and went to Midnight Mass with the family. During the night he had a severe seizure, went into cardiac arrest in the ambulance and died. Liz, her husband and children were deeply grieved.

Liz was always a social activist. She has belonged to the Catholic Women's League for more than fifty years, serving as President and in other offices. She started Birthright in Sarnia in the 1970s and speaks fondly of desperate girls she was able to help. She did not hesitate to speak to the parents of frightened pregnant teens, and she found supportive families to take in these girls during their pregnancies. Under her direction, Birthright kept a downtown office for many years in order that people could walk in discreetly off the street. She recalls doing lots of listening and praying.

Liz had heard about the Third Order while growing up in Ireland and held it in high regard. As an adult, she attended Franciscan retreats and felt drawn to the subdued spirituality, the quiet and depth to Franciscan prayerfulness. When she learned that the Order was starting up locally, she joined at once.

After becoming a Secular Franciscan, Liz, along with her husband, served on the Board of St. Francis Advocates, an organization for autistic adults. Liz took a personal interest in one of the young autistic women in the first SFA residence. More recently, she has travelled to Haiti several times, planting trees and painting schools with the Rayjon mission.

Liz is a widow now. She is comforted by the fact that her husband practiced his Catholic faith during his lifetime and died in grace. As an aside, she commented that he always prayed in Irish. He had the good fortune to die at home, nursed by his wife. On one occasion during his terminal illness, he pulled Liz over and gave her a kiss. Since their father was not overtly demonstrative of affection, a daughter who witnessed the event shared the experience with her sister. The young women wept with the knowledge that their mother had received this belated gift from their father.

Six of Liz's seven children are now married and there are several grandchildren. The offspring are adventurous like their parents and have been all over the world with their various pursuits in teaching, technology, mining and business.

When Liz visited Ireland seven years ago for a nephew's ordination, she heard many unfamiliar family stories from her siblings. It occurred to her, she laments, that despite the busyness of her childhood, her parents had not shared personal information with the family. Since such sharing would have greatly enriched the lives of Liz and her siblings, she's relieved that her own children are more knowledgeable about their family history.

Liz shrugs off the health issues that have cropped up in recent years. She has had surgeries for rare metastatic stromal tumours and is under medical care for this and other health conditions. Nonetheless, she does her own housework and walks to Mass most days.

She has no regrets about her life and describes herself as a happy, content woman. She's glad she persevered in marriage despite some difficulties, and is pleased that the children turned out so well. She prays for her sons, daughters and grandchildren that they will value the Church as she does. Since she has always placed her trust in God, she will continue to do so for them.

Liz is a deeply spiritual person who is welcoming, humble, caring, and has a great sense of humour. Her introverted, intuitive personality takes naturally to prayer, meditation and reflection. She reads extensively, has participated in Ignatian and Franciscan retreats, spent time at Combermere, and visited Roman catacombs as well as shrines in Ireland, the United States and Canada. She has a remarkable gift for quoting from theological sources and can be counted on to contribute words of profound wisdom at Fraternity meetings.

Her mantra has always been, "Sacred Heart of Jesus I place my trust in thee". She added that St.

Bonaventure, in his *Life of St. Francis*, wrote that when the friars asked him to teach them to pray, Francis said, "When you pray, say 'Our Father' and 'We adore you, O Christ, in all your churches in the world and we bless you because by your holy cross you have redeemed the world.'" [1]

She enjoys the story of St Francis seeking permission of the Pope for his Rule and Order.[3] He already had a group of followers, she noted, and could have depended on himself, but he was obedient to the Church and wanted the approval of the Church. She feels that women have a great role to play in the Church "as being women". Jesus had a great respect for women as is seen in his numerous encounters with women, she adds.

IV

MARY

Mary became a Secular Franciscan because she was looking for the next step in her spiritual growth. She believes the seed was planted in her childhood. Whenever her mother would leave the house, she would move the statue of St. Anthony of Padua from the fridge top to the kitchen table and ask the saint to look after things while she was gone.

She was born and raised in the Ottawa Valley with three brothers and one sister. All of her siblings became professionals, her sister became a nun and one brother became a priest.

Their red-headed Irish mother had been a teacher, first teaching in 1920. She read and sang to her children and taught them to pray. She was very active in school, church and community activities, a woman who taught life lessons from day to day. She sent donations to missionaries in foreign lands with left-over change. Mary recalls that her mother's "spiritual gifts of charity and love were shared with all the neighbours and on some occasions when the priest had to be called in for the dying". She was the first to visit immigrants in the area with a cake and a welcoming smile.

In those days, people were waked in their homes. On one occasion, Mary remembers accompanying her mother as she made the rounds of homes in mourning after a hundred people died in the Almonte train wreck, many from her area. Mary's mother practiced temperance, and only as an adult, did Mary realize that her father had been an alcoholic.

Mary's French Canadian father, an energetic labourer, had worked in an aircraft factory during the war and had also been a trapper and hunter. As a boy, he had interacted with aboriginals who taught him to value nature, to hunt only for food, and how to scale and filet fish. Mary remembers that her father kept his catch of fish outside in a galvanized tub of water, chiseling out frozen fish on winter mornings. The family always had fresh fish, venison, pork, beef and delicious baked goods prepared by their mother.

The children practiced their Catholic faith to the letter, attending Catholic grade school with Sisters of the Holy Cross and taught by Sisters of St. Joseph Academy in high school. After graduating as a nurse from St. Vincent de Paul Hospital in Brockville, Mary returned home.

She was immediately hired for the new Annex designed for the rehabilitation of stroke patients. Mary enjoyed working there and began dating and enjoying the friendship of a young doctor. Nonetheless, when a nurse friend accepted a position at the hospital in Mount Forest, Mary decided to go with her to experience further opportunities. She loved the old hospital, the people and the town.

One day a nurse with a teenaged daughter offered to introduce Mary to the "handsome, new, Catholic" French teacher. Sometime later she received a phone call from him asking for a date. Since she was not free at the time, he invited her to chaperone with him at a high school dance.

Mary found the young man polite, a little shy and very likeable. The couple dated often. As the school year came to a close, he wanted to teach closer to home and asked her to leave with him. Subsequently they became engaged and both obtained new positions, she at a Chatham hospital, he at the Harrow high school. They married the following summer in August 1958 and the following year moved to Belle River where her husband taught at his old high school.

The couple were delighted to adopt a baby boy in 1961. Two years later, after a surprise pregnancy that ended in miscarriage, they adopted a second boy. The infant, a sickly baby who had been in two foster homes by the age of six weeks, was welcomed with love. A daughter was born two years later, and a third son in another five years. Mary says her four children gave her many joys.

However, Mary, who loved dances and parties, discovered with the first child that there would be no more partying for her. While her husband went to teachers' parties, took advanced degrees and participated in numerous sports activities, she stayed at home with the children. When they moved into a beautiful new house in 1969, her husband was seldom home. It was Mary who mowed the lawn and made ice rinks for the children. Her only holiday was an annual retreat from which she always returned feeling "light and stress-free". She longed to share the experience with her husband but found him disinterested.

The real suffering in her life began in early 1970. Shortly after the birth of her fourth child, her mother died. Leaving the two oldest children with friends and the newborn with her doctor's wife (who had six children of her own), Mary took the train to Toronto accompanied by her five-year-old daughter. Her priest brother met them at Toronto and they travelled together to join their bereaved family.

When her brother drove her home after the funeral, they found her husband chairing a curling tournament with a female friend. Mary's brother attended the event and encouraged his sister to do so, but she was grieving for her mother and felt the children needed her. Mary now realizes that, by that time, her husband was already involved with female friends.

Living in ignorance, yet feeling increasingly isolated, she cared for her children and meticulously washed and ironed for her husband. Later she tuned out his hints at wanting to leave. But she could not ignore the middle-of-the-night phone call from a man who asked if she knew where her husband was. Despite the hour, Mary replied that he was golfing. The man quietly told her that he felt she should know that her husband was with his daughter. Despite confronting her husband when he finally tiptoed in, shoes in hand, she numbly continued to wash, cook and clean for him. She had no one to confide in, and had been brought up to "always wear lipstick" and look up to her husband. She felt undereducated, had little self-esteem, thought she knew nothing, and gave herself credit for nothing

Her husband left abruptly when their youngest child was four years old and the oldest, thirteen. He wanted to sell the house and move Mary and the children into an apartment. She refused to comply. She recalls being at church with the children and bursting into tears at the end of Mass during *Amazing Grace*. She wondered how anyone could cause someone so much pain.

She received no money that first year from her husband, surviving on the baby bonus, assistance from her family and the kindness of friends. To make ends meet, she stopped papers, magazines, book clubs as well as telephone service. She says that she had to be taught humility but it took five years to acquire. In December of that first year, when she proudly refused a Christmas box, the man from St. Vincent de Paul left it discreetly inside her front door. It was, in fact, badly needed.

Burying her feelings and thoughts, she immersed herself in childrearing. She attended school plays, basketball and football games, helped with science fair projects, and insisted on homework-before-television while she prepared supper. She kept the children properly dressed, carefully mending all their clothes and accepting second hand clothes from caring people. The family lived mainly on vegetables from her extensive garden and determined canning. She took in boarders, hockey players in winter and crew men laying cable in summer. She cleaned offices and houses. The kids had paper routes.

On her first full-time job as a single parent she was scolded and degraded regularly. Feeling hurt and unloved, she would come home from work and weep. Her daughter would try to comfort her. At night, she suffered severe headaches, moaning until her daughter, and sometimes a son, would come in to massage her neck and shoulders. One of her sons feeling rejected first by his biological parents and then by his adopting father, was "crushed beyond words". Although highly intelligent, he began to do badly at school and later turned to drugs. During this terrible time, Mary's mother and siblings prayed for her constantly. Mary believes it was prayer that kept her sane. After the first year, her husband's wages were garnisheed and things became a little easier.

Five years passed and she had a revelation. When the children left for a trip with their father, his mother and his mistress, Mary said goodbye and didn't cry after they left. In fact, she realized that she felt happy for them all. That's when her life started to clear. As she healed, she saw everything differently. She attended 'Beginning Experience' and learned that she had to discover who she was. The first assignment was to go home and list ten things good about oneself. For a week she thought and thought, but couldn't get past the fifteen years of ugliness, pain, and prison-like existence. Finally she wrote that she thought she had nice feet. Other people had to tell her that her cheerfulness and smile were her gifts.

She scanned the course-book from cover to cover as soon as she received it. She read about being a doormat and a martyr, and felt that she had lived the entire book. She began to awaken as if from a fog. A school psychologist, librarian neighbourhood, nun counselor, friends and family gave her books on psychology, self-help, positive thought, enthusiasm and spirituality. She read voraciously, discovering that one can learn more from mistakes than from successes.

Mary began to see how hard she had been on herself and her children. She realized that she was a yeller. She began to keep journals, recording her experiences and insights. In reading over past journals, she can see that while she was "weeping, in hell, persecuted, so worthless, unlovable, exhausted and humiliated", she was attaining much growth. She was being taught humility, patience, compassion, understanding and how to love. She hopes that those who don't want to hear the things she has to say may someday benefit by reading her journals.

She can relate to other people because she has lived it. When her husband's now-second-wife died of cancer, she attended the wake with her children. Seeing him sitting alone and dejected, she felt prompted to send the children to sit with their dad. Encouraged to do so by her nun sister, she acquired an annulment. The process forced her to reflect on her marriage and life. Although incredibly painful, it "reinforced who I am". Mary wonders how it affected her daughter who typed the many pages of information.

From 1986 to 1994 she worked at the local hospital as a nurse. When she retired, her priest brother stayed with her during his terminal illness. She was greatly affected by his death, but began volunteering the following year. She started feeding patients at a city hospital, then did home-visiting for the VON. She now volunteers at the local hospital five hours a week.

When the time was right, the children were older, and life had become more settled, Mary began seeking "something more". She joined the Secular Franciscans in 1989 and was professed in 1991. She wanted simplicity and balance in her life but was afraid of change. She prayed to the Holy Spirit to take away her nervousness, grant her a change of heart, and allow her to grow closer to Christ. She discovered that she could look at her beautiful house and furnishings as having no importance. In 1998 she sold her house and suddenly felt open and free.

Mary says that being a Secular Franciscan has taught her how to simplify her life by knowing what to value. It has shown her how to forget self, reach out to others and distinguish wants from needs. She believes in the power of community and sacraments to nurture growth. Somewhere she read that in the sacrament of reconciliation one should ask forgiveness for all the times you didn't ask for forgiveness in the past. She says that she has learned to see material things as having no importance.

Today Mary lives in a pleasant apartment overlooking the town park and creek. Pictures of her parents, children and grandchildren are proudly displayed. After living in fear and anxiety most of life, she now has a peace that she never had before.

While doing bible study and wondering where to go for love, she looked up "love" in the scriptures, and found the Holy Trinity. Since then the Holy Spirit leads and consoles her. She desires to surrender herself to God's will and share more with community but feels that she is still not there. Everything in life is a lesson, she reflects.

Mary can relate to the story of Francis standing

before the Bishop and handing over his clothes to return to his father.[4] "Francis was now part of Christ's house, not his father's house," she said. "That's where I am now."

V

JOY AND MARTIN

Joy was born in 1933 during the depression. While her parents were living in Detroit, her father found work in Cincinnati almost five hundred miles away. Pregnant with Joy, her mother stayed with her sister. As the due date approached, she got on a bus for Cincinnati but only got as far as Lima where she delivered the baby. Joy's father, expecting a boy, wanted to call her David. Her mother liked the name, Mary. As a compromise, they named their new baby after the hospital in which she was born.

When the family moved to Royal Oak, Joy attended school at the famous shrine of the Little Flower from where Father Charles Caughlin broadcasted his radio programs. Enjoying studies of governments, social encyclicals, social justice and labour issues, she grew up with the desire to go out and change the world. For five years, she worked out of Cleveland and Detroit for Eastern airlines in the reservation department, enjoying trips around the United States on her free air miles. Following this, she was a flight attendant stationed in New York, Boston, Tampa and Miami.

In her late twenties, she became active in the Legion of Mary, visiting homes and giving religious instructions to fallen away Catholics. It was at a Legion of Mary meeting that she met Martin, who had joined the Legion while taking care of his folks in Florida. Previously, Martin had been in a Capuchin monastery in Brazil for ten years studying for the priesthood. He had been refused admission to an American monastery because his brother had been convicted - wrongly, the family believes - of treason for acting as a Nazi translator during his captivity as a German prisoner of war. When his brother's sentence came up for parole, Martin was called upon to testify on his behalf. It happened that at the same time, Pope Pius XII made an edict stating that any seminarian who wavered in his vocation or took time off could not become a priest. Even though Martin was absent from his monastery for the purpose of providing family support, he was not permitted to resume his studies.

Martin and Joy became friends, and after a solemn engagement of one year, were married in 1962 by Father Caughlin at the shrine of the Little Flower. Joy was twenty-nine and Martin was twenty years older.

The idealistic couple wanted to serve the Lord and change the world for Christ. In the first year of marriage, they worked in Indian missions in Prince George, British Columbia. Their first child was born there and baptized by the bishop. They returned to the United States where Martin taught school in Nevada and later worked as director of lay apostolacy in Michigan.

During a subsequent year of unemployment, the family collected discarded food and lived in a cabin on Joy's mother's property. They moved again when Martin obtained work with the unemployment office in Pontiac, Michigan. Their three children attended Catholic school there. But the couple longed to return to the aboriginal mission. Having received an inheritance from Martin's mother, and scandalized by American politics at the time of Watergate, they returned to Canada. They bought a house on Lakeshore Road in Sarnia with the intention of saving enough money to return with their family to the missions.

Martin became a counselor at the Michigan employment security commission. Joy opened the Stella Maris Shop, selling rosaries and other Catholic items and books. People from the Point Edward holy hour helped set it up. The holy hour, overseen by a local Monsignor, was frequented by "Baysiders and Rougements" who were excited over sightings of the Blessed Virgin at Bayside, Michigan. Feeling lost in a Church without Latin, Joy was happy to find something to motivate her spirituality, and took her own children to Bayside.

Since religious processions were common in Michigan, Joy's holy hour friends decided to have a procession down Christina Street in Sarnia. When London's Bishop said no to the project, the group contacted a Toronto Bishop, who readily said yes. Naïvely, they put handouts in all area parishes, Joy and her children handing out flyers after Mass at her church. The parish priest was furious and told Joy's children to get out of the parish. Joy was very upset but the procession went ahead and was well attended. The monsignor was the only priest to attend. The parish priest then came to Joy's shop, demanding that she either swear allegiance to the local bishop or close the Stella Maris. Joy readily agreed to follow the priest's directions and her relationship with him became amiable.

During this time, Joy was unaware that her children were having trouble at school. They were being ridiculed as "bible bangers" and taunted with jeers of "Yankee, go home!" The situation worsened when Joy began suffering from mental illness. As she explains, she was "plagued through her kids' teenage years with four mental breakdowns." Now the youngsters endured hearing about their "crazy mother with the crazy store." They no longer wanted to go to church or to even be Catholic.

The Stella Maris continued in Sarnia for thirty-three years in three locations. Somehow Martin and

Joy never made it back to the aboriginal missions.

Martin joined the local Secular Franciscans as soon as the Fraternity was restored and the first new members were professed in the Order. At that time he had already belonged to the Third Order for thirty-five years. From the start, he was eager to help the Fraternity in any way and assume any office that was given him. He had a wonderful sense of humour and was modest and humble, never bringing up his advanced theological background.

Joy became a member two years later "to draw closer to Martin." She was just recovering from a breakdown, and says she has no memory of the formation period. A Franciscan priest cautioned her to postpone her profession, and she did for a brief time. Joy always had a deep devotion to the Blessed Mother and to the Eucharist. However, when idealistic Martin talked about Franciscan poverty, his more realistic wife replied that they had bills to pay.

Over the years, Joy has grown very fond of the Order. She now prays regularly to Saints Francis and Clare, has a much better idea of fraternity and truly appreciates her Franciscan brothers and sisters. In fact, she wishes they would get together more often than once a month. She finds the ongoing formation at each gathering meaningful and informative, filling in the memory blanks from her initial formation.

When Martin died in the spring of 2000, the local fraternity planned and conducted his wake service. Joy recalls the brown Franciscan scapular worn by her husband, his well-attended funeral and the violinist at the graveside. Joy is happy that Martin received a certificate marking his fifty years in the Order before he died and that he has two memorial stones dedicated to him at the Washington retreat house, one from her and one from the Fraternity.

Joy struggled to keep her shop running for more than five years after her husband's death. He had been her dedicated business partner for many years. Now after a year of retirement, she's had a chance to pray and reflect at length. She says that prayer was the only solid thing she knew when she was forced to close her shop and sell her house. She goes weekly for her hour of adoration at the Eucharistic Chapel and prays to the Holy Spirit for guidance and inspiration. She is trying to select meaningful scripture passages for her children to hear at her funeral. Her favorite is the discourse where Christ says *whoever eats my flesh and drinks my blood*..."and people walked away". She's looking for something special in St. Paul showing Jesus being loving.

With the grace of God, she learned to manage things and had no more breakdowns after age sixty. But she was depressed and anxious over her children's leaving the Church. With her current year of prayer drawing to a close, Joy has come to believe that God does not damn people for leaving the Church. She believes something good will happen during their lifetimes that will bring them to see the truth of Catholicism. Her four children, still unmarried, are very good people. They all believe in God, care about ecology, and trust in God for good things in their lives.

Joy is grateful that she has a good relationship with her children. She regularly talks and prays with them. She is heartened that they are not involved in the rat race and that they desire quiet stress-free lives. She wonders aloud about the Stella Maris. An old priest once asked her how she could run her business and take care of a family too. "Did my high profile and busyness have an adverse effect on my children? Was there no time for fun?" she muses. "My own parents worked very hard and had no time for fun."

Joy has always been a reflective person. She feels that Pope John Paul II believed that the Church is coming into a new Pentecostal birth that she won't live to see. She comments that young people are hungering for spirituality and need Catholic models to inspire them. She relates that Gandhi said he would have become a Christian if he had ever met one. Joy says that she hasn't met many Catholics of the younger generation who are sufficiently fervent, and that so many have fallen into materialism.

She thinks sadly of all the lives that were created for a purpose and won't be there because of abortion. "What an insult to God!" She tells an anecdote where someone asks God, "Why haven't you sent us a new Abraham Lincoln?" God replies: "I did but you aborted him."

Young people, she says, are the ones who will go

forth with the Gospel and change the world. She prays for that and for the peace that our Lady of Fatima promised when she foretold of future turmoil and said that in the end her Immaculate Heart will triumph and mankind will be granted an era of peace. But she feels that today's children have neither an awe for the sacrifice of the Mass or the knowledge of graces obtained from sacraments. They lack teachings on such things as vestments and saints, she notes, and everyone has lost a sense of sin.

Joy prays to St. Clare every night that she can follow Mary's life. "She was conceived without sin so she must have been wise, intelligent and virtuous. But she had grace to know what her role was in life. She never stepped beyond what God called her to do as I often did in my life," she adds. No doubt Martin would remind Joy that, despite bumps along the way, she has remained faithful to their goal as newlyweds: to serve the Lord and change the world for Christ.

Joy likes the story about Francis and the friar being denied admission to a monastery, a story of perfect joy.[5] It appeals to her sense of humour and to her appreciation of Francis' gift for illuminating a moral in such a delightful way. As well, Joy has learned through the trials of her life that joy comes when it is least expected.

VI

LLOYD

Lloyd's journey to Catholicism and then to Franciscanism was travelled via a long, winding route. But God was along for the trek. Although Lloyd describes himself as having a Type A personality, he comes across as a quiet, thoughtful person. Friendly and likeable, he has provided organized leadership to our Fraternity, expressing good ideas and listening attentively to the opinions of others.

Lloyd comes from a people rooted in prairie farming. His father was the first in the family to leave the farm, becoming an aircraft mechanic in the armed forces in World War II. One of Lloyd's earliest recollections is of sleeping in a dresser drawer on an army base in Manitoba. He also remembers wearing a brown dress coat with big brown buttons. He describes his family as average, "neither big communicators nor big on affection". Although they were members of the United Church, they seldom attended church services. After the war, his father worked for Massey Ferguson until he retired. Lloyd has one brother and two sisters. He has always loved prairie farms and camping.

He started school in Saskatoon, then moved to Ontario at the end of the fifth grade. He found the curriculum in his new school to be behind that of Saskatoon's. It was like repeating a grade, he says. In Toronto, Lloyd had a superb twelfth grade chemistry teacher who instilled in him a permanent love of chemistry. He studied sciences at university in London, choosing chemistry over engineering and attaining a PhD. While waiting for confirmation of a job with IBM, he was hired sooner by Imperial Oil and moved to Sarnia. Four years in the plant's research department was followed by four in the chemical plant inspection lab. He then moved with his family to Baton Rouge, Louisiana, where he was employed for two years in polyethylene technology before returning to Sarnia.

Married in 1963, he had four children with his first wife. The family belonged to the United Church where the children attended Sunday school. In his late thirties, Lloyd began searching for more inner depth with less focus on day-to-day routine. Spirituality started to come alive for him.

Initially, the family found spiritual nourishment in

the Anglican Church. But during their time in Baton Rouge, they found the Louisiana Episcopal Church to be more like a social club. They investigated the Catholic Church, and found the traditions and solidity more to their liking. 'Faith of Our Fathers' is a powerful hymn that speaks most clearly for Catholicity, Lloyd states.

Back in Sarnia, he was introduced to Cursillo. It made a great difference in his faith life. He helped start a folk choir in his parish and participated on 'Christ in Others Retreat' (COR) teams, organizing inspirational Christian weekends for young people.

Lloyd admires the Catholic Church for "not whipping in the wind" as do other churches today. There are things he would like to see changed, but change for the Church is slow, he notes. Also, he believes there are too many rules, and one should be guided more by faith than rules. Nonetheless, he remains cheerfully committed to the Church. Religious practice helped him through divorce in 1986. In his distress, he prayed, asking God to let the painful situation go God's way. Putting circumstances in God's hands, Lloyd felt the anxiety fading away, and over time, it did work out God's way.

Lloyd first met his current wife in choir, next at 'Beginning Experience', and then everywhere he seemed to go. The couple seemed destined for each other and married in 1988. They have similar personalities, values and interests. Between them, they have seven adult children whom they truly enjoy.

Believing in God has never been a problem for Lloyd. He cannot understand how a scientist, with the knowledge he has, can be an atheist. He believes that most scientists are believers. The structure of the world cannot be random, he points out. A scientist who can believe that nothing directs the forces of creation is not very intelligent, he adds.

It was the admiration St. Francis held for the Creator alive in all of Creation that struck a chord with Lloyd. Fascinated by the saint since he was a child, he attended a Secular Franciscan information meeting in 1991. He and his wife began the Formation process together. Although his wife realized that it was not her calling, she remains supportive to Lloyd's Franciscan journey. Following the Rule of Francis has added a unique Franciscan charism to Lloyd's spirituality. He enjoys the community aspect essential to Franciscanism and finds the meetings quiet, prayerful and powerful.

In 1992, Lloyd was asked to bring his work experience and knowledge to Saudi Arabia. He and his wife lived there for three and a half years. During that time, freedom to practice their faith openly was non-existent, but following the Rule of his Order remained part of Lloyd's life. Occasionally Masses were held secretly in private Catholic homes.

When the couple travelled outside Saudi Arabia, they were sometimes able to attend Mass publicly. In the United Emirates, a sheik had built a Catholic church and school next door to a huge mosque.

Isolated from the modern world, Mass there was like going back to the Middle Ages. People indeed seemed to be worshipping statues, and Lloyd felt that persons of other faiths could certainly get the wrong impression. A more positive experience occurred in Malaysia one Christmas morning. Mass was beautiful. However, they walked out the front door of the cathedral to the sound of construction cranes. Christmas was not observed as a holy day in mostly-Muslim Malaysia. Some people in the country are, in fact, trying to implement sharia law.

In 1998, Lloyd volunteered to go back to Saudi Arabia for some major projects. During this time, his wife chose to remain living in Canada and to visit him in Saudi Arabia from time to time. She had found the Muslim culture too oppressive, especially to women, during their first long stay. After this assignment, Lloyd decided to retire.

Lloyd uses an example from Islam to support his own attitude toward his spiritual journey. In Mohammed's day, the leaders of a mosque were making their midday prayers longer and longer. Since Muslims pray five times a day, people complained to Mohammed that they were being detained too long in the mosque. Mohammed called the leaders and reminded them that each prayer was meant to be a certain length. Midday prayer, as defined in the Koran, was to be short.

Being a Secular Franciscan calls for us to follow the Rule of the Order. It is not required, nor even wise, notes Lloyd, to feel obliged to add the devotions of other spiritual movements. Extensive periods of prayer are appropriate in a monastery. Each lay person must listen to his own soul when communicating with God. The world is a complex place requiring of Jesus' servants prayerfulness, common sense, a listening ear and an open heart. These qualities, quietly alive in Lloyd, are as applicable to our Franciscan fraternity as they are to the communities of family, parish, town or city. Lloyd says that the story of Francis and the wolf of Gubbio came alive for him when he became aware that the wolf was probably someone who was terrorizing his community.[6]

VII

ELIZABETH

Because Elizabeth had always been a gentle person, it took us a while to realize that she was becoming increasingly withdrawn. At Fraternity meetings, she no longer shared the depth of wisdom and spirituality that we had come to enjoy. Her easy laughter faded into a distant smile. She lightly dismissed inquiries into her well-being. When she was invited to speak during our sharing circles, she would say that she really liked what the others had said and had nothing to add. We worried about her memory lapses and, initially, we suspected that she was depressed or carrying a secret burden. When she told us that her son now had her car, Fraternity members began picking her up for meetings and gatherings.

Finally we learned that she had been diagnosed with Alzheimer's disease. With typical courage and good-natured acceptance, Elizabeth told us that she was taking a new drug that promised to give her three years of mostly normal life. And indeed, the Elizabeth we knew seemed to return – for a while. But all too quickly, the three years passed. Soon she could no longer remain at home, even with her family's assistance. For a time, she lived with a son in Toronto, but after a while, she was placed in a nursing home.

When St. Anthony of Padua Fraternity was reactivated in 1983 after twenty-five years of dormancy, Elizabeth had been among the first nine postulants to heed the call of Jesus through following Francis of Assisi. How blessed we are to have had her journeying with us these many years.

Recently, her sister-in-law, Ann, and I met with Elizabeth to put together some of her remarkable story. She welcomed us warmly, admitting that she couldn't quite come up with our names. She led us down the halls of the bright modern building she now calls home, but actually, it was Ann who was able to locate Elizabeth's room.

Elizabeth grew up on a farm near Mount Carmel with ten siblings. At age sixteen she began working with Northern Telecom in London and then for London Life. She met her husband-to-be at a baseball game where he was the star pitcher for the Exeter Mohawks. The couple married at Mount Carmel in 1954 with their reception held at Grand Bend. Elizabeth was twenty-one at the time, her husband twenty-two. Two daughters were born in London followed by two sons.

During this time, Elizabeth's husband worked for Canadian National Railways until he had a stroke from which he slowly recovered. Unable to continue in his former employment, he went back to school and received a teaching certificate in shop. The young family moved to Leamington in 1965 where her husband secured a position as a high school shop teacher. To supplement his income during the summer months, he worked as a welder in the Windsor CN yards. A year after moving to Leamington, a third son was born. Three years later, the busy family moved to a house in the country.

In 1972 while returning home from his railway yard job, Elizabeth's husband died in a car accident. It was his fortieth birthday. Elizabeth found herself with five children to raise alone. The oldest child was fifteen and the youngest five. When her husband's brother and his wife, Ann, invited her to join them in Sarnia, Elizabeth moved her belongings and children once again. At the time, two of Elizabeth's brothers also lived in Sarnia.

Shortly after she moved to Sarnia, Elizabeth made a Cursillo weekend with Ann. It had a tremendous impact on both women. For Elizabeth, it was a welcome source of spiritual strength and awakening. She went on to serve on many Cursillo teams, including a stint as Rector. It was in a small weekly Cursillo prayer group that I got to know Elizabeth and Ann personally.

In the late 1970s, Elizabeth became involved with Lambton Right to Life. It remained her passion until her illness necessitated retirement. For years, the Right to Life phone listing was her home number. In time there was an office manned by other volunteers, but Elizabeth was frequently on duty there. In line with her pro-family concerns, for many years Elizabeth retained the volunteer position of Treasurer for the Christian Heritage Party.

With her family growing up, Elizabeth began working outside her home. She did test driving for Esso and prepared income taxes for H & R Block.

In the mid-1980s, shortly after we had begun to study the ways of the Saint of Assisi, I turned to Elizabeth for help. There was a desperate need in the area for services for autistic adolescents, my son being one of these. Elizabeth's response was immediate and unconditional. She and her sister-in-law, Ann, worked diligently with me through several difficult years in creating St. Francis Advocates, an organization devoted to autistic persons. Elizabeth became its first President.

Elizabeth's oldest son recently commented that his mother could be emotionally distant. Certainly, Elizabeth has always been quiet, self-effacing and undemonstrative, but she always spoke of her children with tremendous pride and concern. She was very conscientious of their religious upbringing, attendance at Mass and Catholic education. Perhaps the burden of being a single parent drained her of the energy necessary to communicate her feelings to the children she held so dear.

To their family's credit, Elizabeth's children have grown into fine adults. Her older daughter directs a children's music program at Humber College in

Toronto. The other daughter is busy raising two daughters of her own. The oldest of her three sons is married and studying to become a process operator. A second son is a project manager for BP in Houston. The youngest son, a high school teacher in Toronto, has a boy and girl.

Elizabeth: true friend, cheerful provider of encouragement, protector of the vulnerable, modest and humble. She has always loved the life and spirituality of the Secular Franciscan Order, delighting in the prayers and stories associated with Francis and Clare. Elizabeth's life exemplifies the Franciscan call to simplicity. Each of the Order's branches addresses Poverty in their Rules.[7]

VIII

SIMONE

Simone joined our Secular Franciscan Fraternity in the spring of 1997 and was professed in the autumn of 1999. She took Agnes of Assisi, sister of St. Clare, as her patron because she "didn't feel worthy of the name, Clare". She appreciates the fraternity and says it "feels like one heart", each member having the same longing for God. Compared to the depth of conversations with Franciscans, she says, other conversations seem vague and empty. In her typically humble manner, she marvels at how fraternity members respect what she contributes and "act like I say something special."

Simone is the second oldest in a family of eleven. The oldest child died when he was fifteen days old, and a second brother died at age twenty-one. Their mother was a severe woman unable to demonstrate affection or gentleness. She, in turn, had been raised by Quebec pioneers who cleared their own land, sleeping in a wagon until their first cabin was built. The children were fearful of their father. They walked five miles to school in summer and stayed home the remainder of the year.

As well as being critical and complaining, Simone's mother showed favouritism. A sister who wet the bed ate apart from the rest of the family and was made to sleep in unwashed sheets. Her father, who would not openly challenge his wife, secretly asked the girl if she wished to be sent to relatives. The girl declined.

The family went to church every Sunday and were taught by nuns. They valued the traditional teachings and devotions. Simone herself wished to become a nun until she discovered boys. In the early years, the family prayed the rosary every evening and listened to Cardinal Leger on radio. The advent of television replaced both.

Simone was often punished for disagreeing with her mother. Although she did lots of work around the house and farm, she refused to quit school as her mother demanded. A younger sister bowed to her mother's will, left school in Grade seven, and completed her education as a married woman with four children.

Despite her harsh upbringing, Simone loves her parents. She regrets that her mother has not involved herself with the lives of her grown children or any of her grandchildren.

Simone left home at age twenty. She had wanted to become a teacher until the local teachers' college closed. Unable to afford training at a more distant place, she moved to Montreal where she worked as a receptionist in a publishing house.

There she met her future husband who, at the age of eighteen, had escaped from a communist country. She was captivated with his beautiful, sad eyes, his longing for his homeland and his talk of a loving grandmother. She saw him as more mysterious than the village boys back home and knew she would marry him. Whenever he was late, Simone feared that he had returned to his homeland.

The young man told her that there were three requirements for the woman he would marry. First, she was not to work outside the home, because he had hated coming home to an empty house while his own mother worked. Secondly, if his parents ever came to Canada, they would live with him, and thirdly, there could be no diaper rash on any of their babies.

Simone readily agreed to his conditions. Nonetheless, the couple did not get married for four years by which time there was a child. Because of her poor relationship with her mother, Simone prayed at St. Joseph's Oratory for sons rather than daughters. In time, she had three sons, and now thinks that a daughter would have been nice.

Over time, three of her husband's four siblings also escaped from their communist homeland, and each time his family was penalized with alienation and demotions. Later, when her mother-in-law visited two of her sons in Montreal, Simone wondered why the woman cried so much. Her mother had not even wept at her own son's funeral.

Simone's mother-in-law was a journalist in her country. She thanked Simone for marrying her son and offered to care for her grandchildren even though it would necessitate separation from her husband over there. She felt that the family would benefit financially if her daughter-in-law could work. The couple declined the offer.

On one occasion, Simone sent a letter written in French to her mother-in-law knowing that she could have it translated into her own language. Last year, as the elderly woman lay dying, Simone felt prompted by the Holy Spirit to send her another letter. However, by the time she got around to writing, it was almost too late. The letter arrived when the dying woman was in a coma. She rallied briefly as the letter was read to her and then slipped again into unconsciousness. Simone hopes she was able to hear her words of love and gratitude.

Simone and her family moved to Sarnia, Ontario twenty-four years ago. Her husband, by then a truck driver, was often away, leaving her responsible for child rearing and household management. While studying English as a second language, she met a woman who listened to her problems and was interested in what she had to say. The woman was like a mother to her, the mother she felt she never had. They became best friends.

At one point in her life, as she struggled with her marriage, her friend counseled her to 'let it go'. It took Simone five or six years to bring about change in herself. By this time, she and her friend were Secular Franciscans. Gradually she learned to let go of her pain by focusing on the Peace Prayer attributed to Francis. *O Divine Master, Grant that I may not so much seek: to be consoled, as to console; to be understood, as to understand; to be loved, as to love.*

Another struggle was learning to adjust to visits by her husband's family. Initially, when her husband and sister discussed their childhood in their native tongue, she felt ignored and hurt. Now that she has better understanding of the language, she participates in these conversations. She has also grown comfortable at leaving them to their reminiscing.

In 1994, Simone and her husband were consecrated to Mary. The Blessed Mother took over her life. Simone believes in Mary's promise that if you go astray, she will put you back on track before you die. She says her husband also has a strong faith. He prays in his own language, explaining that it means more to him. Upon learning to pray in her husband's language, Simone led a Cenacle on Saturday nights which her husband attended for four or five years.

After she and her husband returned from Marmora, he was insistent that he must go to confession. Finally, he related to her that while meditating at the Tenth Station of the Cross at Marmora, all the sins of his past life had been revealed to him. From an indiscretion at age five, he had been able to see the domino effect of sin. He insisted on going to a priest in Windsor. Simone says that perhaps she wasn't shown her sins because it would be too frightening.

She strives for holiness, noting that Mother Theresa said that it is a great loss and failure to not seek holiness. She notes that too many people use issues in the Church as an excuse to not practice their faith. After all, the Church is the people. "Whenever there were bad times in the Church," she says, "saints like St. Francis came along to straighten it out."

She loves nature and sees Francis there. In her garden, surrounded by flowers, a statue of Mary stands atop an arrangement of flagstones. Simone says she has a more beautiful statue in her bedroom, but the garden one, hand-painted by a friend, is "lovely from a distance".

Simone can get tears in her eyes from hearing birds sing or feeling the wind upon her skin. She passionately believes that "every man deserves a piece of land", that "a tree is the most precious thing", and that "nature is therapeutic for anyone".

Simone loves her sons and their families and hopes that God will be important in their lives. She is happy that her granddaughter was baptized Catholic and that the priest consecrated all the babies to Mary during the rite that day. She wonders what her role should be toward her one son's foster children, one of whom is "Christian", the other Jewish.

With her wit, warmth and sparkle, Simone truly brings the joy of Francis to all she meets. Genuinely caring and concerned about each member, she enriches our Secular Franciscan fraternity with the essence of Christian community.

Devoted to Mary, Simone is drawn to the prayers of St. Francis to the Blessed Mother of Jesus.[8]

IX

CECILIA

Cecilia was the fifth of sixteen children born in Quebec to a very devout Catholic family. She was educated by nuns and from her earliest years felt called to be a nun. She was always in the convent helping the nuns who taught the poor in the poorest parish. Hers was a truly spiritual environment in which to develop.

After working for two years at a Catholic newspaper, Cecilia entered the novitiate and trained as a teacher. Assigned to a small country parish, she taught large combined classes of grades six to ten. For four years, she worked extremely hard preparing senior multi-grades for government exams.

Three months before her final vows, she became exhausted and ill. The convent's physician said that she should be given her freedom. After the nuns in her convent prayed for her, Mother Superior told Cecilia that, while they felt very badly, they had decided she needed to leave. She was a perfectionist and worked too hard.

Cecilia was devastated. A priest tried to reassure her by explaining that she had had a "temporary religious calling". Initially she didn't want to continue teaching for these nuns but she ended up teaching for them for thirty-one years. The nuns continued to treat her like one of their own, and let her teach the higher grades as she preferred. When her school in Quebec city went from all-girls to co-ed, she was assigned straight Grade 11 mathematics.

God had called her to life in the greater community. Outside school hours, she became involved in the parish with *Jeunesse Ouvriere Catholique*, the young Catholic worker. She founded the Legion of Mary in the parish. In summer, she was hired as assistant director of children, holding this non-paying position for ten years. She raised money through bingos. Every day she rode fifteen kilometres to camp with a busload of girls from poor families. Sometimes she stayed weekends with the camp leaders to help plan activities.

Cecilia lived at home with her parents while she taught in Quebec. Thus she was able to help with the finances when her Father retired in 1965. Her brothers and sisters are all well-educated: four engineers, three nurses, and two government secretaries. Her oldest sister, a nun, told her that her reason for leaving the convent was because their parents needed her.

In 1975, while the youngest of her sisters was pregnant with her second child, the woman's husband had an accident and died. Cecilia's father, who went to Mass every day, said it should have been him in the coffin. He asked Cecilia to accompany him to the Cemetery Office where he paid for ninety-nine years of upkeep on the lot he had purchased in 1945 at the death of his infant son.

Shortly thereafter, her father became ill with a condition his doctor was unable to diagnose. It had always been his custom to bless the family every New Years. As he became increasingly ill and was hospitalized, he asked his children to come to him in small groups for one last blessing. Cecilia was with her father when he died at the age of seventy-five in 1976.

Her mother had osteoporosis and, during hospitalization for pneumonia, had her ribs fractured while being assisted out of bed. She suffered internal bleeding and died December 31, 1978, Cecilia and a nurse-daughter at her side.

In 1980, Cecilia, despite having seniority in the math department, took a sabbatical year to make room for a young male teacher who would otherwise have lost his mathematics teaching position. She decided to use her sabbatical studying English as a second language at Lambton College. There she met two young Vietnamese men, one who had been a teacher in Vietnam. Moved by their situation, Cecilia helped to pay for their education for three years while they studied mechanical engineering and chemistry. When she retired in 1983, she was persuaded by the men to move to Sarnia and allow them to live with her. Four years later, the older Vietnamese man was ready to buy his own house.

Providentially, at the same time, Cecilia's youngest brother requested permission to rent the family home in Quebec which Cecilia had purchased from her siblings when their parents died. Cecilia gave it to him as a wedding gift. She now felt free to remain in Sarnia.

In 1990, the older of the Vietnamese brothers married a Vietnamese princess. By now, Cecilia wanted to return to Quebec to live with a sister who had renovated her house in anticipation of her return. But the family of the Vietnamese brothers pressed her to stay. The oldest brother had sponsored a seventeen-year-old brother in 1984, just prior to father's death. The Vietnamese government retaliated by preventing the young man from attending university and making his mother pay back his tuition money. In 1992, the mother begged the consulate in Thailand to allow her son to immigrate. The Vietnamese government forced the Canadian brother to sponsor his brother, mother and sister. The sister did not want to leave her thriving business or her large family still in Vietnam.

Given no choice, the Vietnamese trio came to

Canada and moved into the oldest son's large house. Cecilia was also living there, having rented out her own house. The princess wife and her in-laws fought endlessly. In 1996, the mother and youngest son, now diagnosed as schizophrenic, returned to Vietnam but were sent back to Canada by the government.

When they returned, they asked to live in Cecilia's currently-rented house. Cecilia moved back with them, adding two more rooms and a bathroom in the basement apartment.

Many who knew Cecilia wondered why she remained so committed to her Vietnamese friends through all their turmoil and troubles. But Cecilia felt that it was her calling to help the people that God placed in her path.

In 1994, she entered the Secular Franciscan Formation process and was professed in 1996. While teaching in Quebec, she had a Capuchin spiritual director, and she had organized a Capuchin pilgrimage with children. At the time, she hoped to become involved with Franciscans but felt unworthy. She was living in the poorest part of town, and the Franciscans were uptown people.

From 1984, her retirement year, until 1997, she drove from Quebec to Florida at the end of every October with a brother, his wife and their daughter who has Down syndrome. She returned by plane and retrieved them again each April. When the brother died, Cecilia went to Florida to help her sister-in-law sell the house and care for her daughter.

It happened that this brother died while Cecilia was in Assisi. She was there on a twenty-eight day pilgrimage, 'In the steps of Francis', with twenty-five nuns and lay people from Montreal and Quebec. Because her brother had cancer of the pancreas, Cecilia had a Mass said for him in St. Clare Basilica before the San Damiano Crucifix. During the night, she heard her name called loudly. She later learned that her brother had died at that very hour. It was early on June 20, 1997.

Cecilia became interested in l'Arche but, in 2004 when the Vietnamese mother died just before she was to return to Vietnam, she decided that her heart was with her Vietnamese people. The Vietnamese family calls Cecilia the "mother of them all". She has been to Vietnam three times and has had expensive clothes lavished on her by the grateful sisters and brother who remain in that country. She says, with an apologetic smile, that she would never spend so much money on herself. Indeed, she spends no money on new things for her house, only necessities.

While in Vietnam, the sister living in Canada had taken Cecilia to Mass every day despite her family being Buddhist. In 1997, the young woman converted to Catholicism. When Cecilia was in Medugorje, she prayed that the woman would find a husband, and in 2006, she married a Catholic widower.

For now, Cecilia is mostly alone in her house with two cats belonging to the now-married Vietnamese sister. She also keeps the woman's dog while its owner works. The schizophrenic brother now divides his time between Cecilia's house and his oldest brother's. Although she often longs to return to Quebec, Cecilia feels obligated to care for the young man, even handling his disability pension, because she is the only one who can control his difficult behaviour.

The next time this young man visits Vietnam, his family hopes he will be able to remain there, receiving treatment in his own country. They apply monthly for his visa. The future is in God's hands, says Cecilia with a smile, adding that her motto is "one day at a time".

Cecilia became closer to Mary during a visit to Fatima in 1979. Since then, her devotion to Mary is very deep. "When I look at my life," she says, "I realize that God is working with me through the people that need my help. All the big decisions in my life are in dealing with someone else's needs." She says that is seems she will only go to Quebec if someone needs her there.

Since 1980, she has travelled extensively. Most of these trips have been pilgrimages. Since her Fatima conversion, she has been five times to Medugorje, twice in the footsteps of Saint Paul through Greece and Turkey, twice in the Holy Land, once to Poland, and, of course, to Assisi. She has been to Haiti seven times with the Rayjon ministry and once to the Dominican Republic. On three occasions she has assisted with the eye glass clinic which provides people with donated prescription glasses for which they pay fifty cents a pair. Volunteers with Rayjon are required to pay their own fare as well as bring the materials they will use there. Cecilia is returning this fall to supervise.

Cecilia trusts in God's providence and the Holy Spirit. She believes that it is God's will for her that there are always people needing attention. For example, she cared for an ill sister who, after a brief family visit in Quebec, returned to Sarnia to be with Cecilia when she died.

For the past five years, she had been taking care of elderly persons in the community. They are often French speaking. Sometimes she is approached by concerned family members who will be away for a while. She visits her charges in apartments and nursing homes, and takes them to doctors' appointments.

She is a Eucharistic minister in her parish, serving Communion at Mass as well as in nursing homes and to the homebound. She has a deep devotion for the Eucharist and is a weekly adorer at the Eucharistic chapel. During Mass she looks at the elevated host at Consecration and says, "My Lord and My God" as Francis' father taught him to do. Cecilia says it was very meaningful for her to have this confirmed in a reading by Julian Green.

Cecilia took me on a tour of her modestly furnished home. In her living room, she showed me a lovely painting given to her by the grateful

Vietnamese family. One room contains a strange collection of gaudy flashing trinkets on which the schizophrenic man spends all his money.

A simple shrine in her own room has flowers and incense sticks arranged before photos of her deceased family members as well as the Vietnamese mother. Cecilia especially likes a unique picture of the Holy Trinity portraying the Son with a look-alike Father who seems to be a kindly, approachable middle-aged figure. The Holy Spirit is shown as a dove. "You and I can relate to a kindly Father because of our backgrounds," she commented. "Not everyone is as fortunate."

Cecilia's brother and sister-in-law will be visiting this summer as will a widowed sister. She relates wryly that she has been at so many family death beds that it has become a family joke that one should be prepared to die when visiting with Cecilia.

Cecilia's family has always lived their faith by example rather than by words. It makes her sad that she is not an evangelizer. She cannot witness verbally but teaches by example, she says. This she does well. In our fraternity, she is the Formation Director, conscientiously attending regional meetings and workshops. She has a particular devotion to the Mother of Perpetual Help and to the Holy Spirit. Everywhere she goes, she is reminded that she is Franciscan. She loves that Francis tried not so much to bring God to the world as to show that God was already there.

She likes many of the Franciscan writings, the stories of Francis with lepers and the wolf, and the *Canticle of Brother Sun.* The letters of Clare to Agnes of Prague, with the image of the mirror, became more meaningful to her when she visited the Church of St. Agnes in Prague. However, because she had a problem with forgiveness over a family problem following her brother's death, Cecilia's selection, cited in the footnotes, is the *Paraphrase of the Our Father* by St. Francis.[9]

X

FRANCES

When I visited Frances in her nursing home, it was apparent that she had deteriorated since my last visit. Although she recognized me and said she had been expecting me, she spoke haltingly in a low voice. Nonetheless, in her typically caring way, she asked how I was and inquired after my family. She then wanted to know how the Fraternity was doing. "Being a Franciscan means everything to me," she said repeatedly during the visit.

When I asked about her own family, she smiled but could not come up with numbers or names. She spoke vaguely of "past tragedies", adding, "That's where God comes into your life." During our time together, she noted that we never think we can get through things, but we do. We keep trying to go on just as we always have. With some prompting, she talked about the enjoyment she and her husband used to have square dancing and round dancing. They had elaborate costumes and travelled extensively to participate in competitions. "It was a lovely way to escape from the cares of the world. We had lots of fun."

Frances talked about missing her husband deeply. "It's been a long time," she said. "I wouldn't know what to do without Saint Francis." She smiled fondly as we talked about her granddaughter who had been one of my hospital volunteers.

Several times she called out to her roommate to see if she was okay. She told me they were two peas in a pod, both bedridden and needing care. Polite and gentle as she has always been, she thanked me numerous times for visiting.

Frances said that she prays all the time and acknowledged that she has an important role in praying for her family, friends and the whole troubled world. Before our visit ended, she took my hand and asked me to bless her.

"Pray for me," she said as I stood to leave. "I pray for all of you."

Like our Frances, the Saint of Assisi relied on intercessory prayer. On once such occasion, St. Francis sent his friend, Brother Masseo, to seek the prayerful counsel of Sister Clare and Brother Sylvester to guide him through a major decision.[10]

I called upon Frances' granddaughter to relate her grandmother's story. Frances was an only child, born and raised in Toronto. Her mother had suffered heart and other health problems as a result of Rheumatic Fever, and the family worked to care for one another as best they could. Her upbringing involved much hardship. Frances' aunt lived with them and helped to care for her as a child. With her father working to support his family and her mother struggling with deteriorating health issues and frequent hospital stays, Frances and Auntie became very close.

Frances watched as her mother struggled with illness and had to say goodbye to her as a young child. She always held a special place in her heart for her mother, but Auntie was also very dear to her. Frances was orphaned as a young adult, when her father died suddenly. Years later, when Auntie's health failed, Frances brought her to live with her family and cared for her until she died. Auntie's death left Frances with no blood relatives and feeling very much alone. In contrast to her small family, Frances' husband came from a rather large family who welcomed her into their clan. She became very close with her brothers and sisters-in-law and came to think of them as her own siblings.

Frances had a love of knowledge. She loved to learn and wanted to help people. She worked in a few secretarial jobs and continued to better herself through courses at community college. She completed a certificate and worked as a health care aide until she retired to raise her children. She was always very proud of her accomplishments and shared her enthusiasm for learning with her family.

Frances met her husband shortly after he came home from the war; they enjoyed a short courtship and married in her early twenties. The couple started their lives together in 1947 in Toronto, ventured to the Western part of Canada and then settled in Southern Ontario. When they arrived in Sarnia, they rented a room until they were able to purchase the home in which they lived in for a number of years. The after effects of the war remained with Frances' husband, but she supported him and offered him comfort from the terrible memories of what he had experienced.

Unable to have children of their own, Frances and her husband opened their hearts and home to two young children needing a family. They adopted their son in 1953 and their daughter in 1960. Frances was a devoted mother, providing unstinting love and support. She was proud of her children and took advantage of her bragging rights at every opportunity.

The couple were members of St. Peter's Church until they became founding members of their neighbourhood parish, St. Benedict. Initially, the parishioners gathered in the gym at St. Patrick's High School. From its birth, Frances was involved with the growth and development of the new parish. She became an active member of the Catholic Women's League, generously volunteering her time to the organization.

Frances and her husband enjoyed square dancing and won many awards for their talent. They traveled to competitions and even coaxed their children into participating in the sport. Frances made and tailored all the costumes for their competitions. In addition to traveling for dance, the couple traveled to visit family, enjoying camping excursions and family reunions.

They cultivated an extensive garden of vegetables and flowers. Frances spent countless hours in the kitchen preparing meals, canning, and baking treats for her family to enjoy. She liked her desserts, chocolate and candies, and insisted that everyone else share the delight.

When Frances' fifth grandchild arrived, she was able to witness the precious arrival of a most special gift of life. Having adopted her own children, she missed the opportunity to share in this beautiful blessing. Frances was thrilled and grateful to be granted this experience.

Frances remained active into her seventies, maintaining active membership at the Strangway Recreation Centre. Visiting with friends and participating in arts and crafts and line dancing were among her favorite activities.

In 1993, Frances came home to find her husband unconscious. A few days later as she sat at his side in intensive care, she once again found herself saying goodbye to someone she held dear. Now widowed after forty-seven years of marriage, she was heartbroken and anxious over the welfare of her other loved ones.

She moved in with her daughter and grandchildren, and although she was surrounded by lots of bustle, she slowly began to distance herself from family and friends. She no longer joined friends in social activities or found joy in things that once brought her pleasure. She continued to care about those who were close to her, but found it too difficult to participate in activities shared with her husband for over forty years.

As Frances entered her late seventies and early eighties, her health began deteriorating and she moved to a nursing home. Until very recently, she was quick and witty and enjoyed making people laugh. "She was usually very modest and reserved, but when she came out with a funny, it was unexpected and it was a good one!" She now experiences frustration as she progressively experiences less mobility and more confusion.

Still, visits from family, friends, church associates and furry pals can brighten her day. Frances had dogs growing up and her love of animals continues. Frances delights in visiting with Esther, the nursing home's pet rabbit, and likes to introduce her visitors to her new buddy. When she feels anxious, the staff often settle her with a visit from Esther.

From her nursing home bed, Frances admitted to her family that, although she has faith in what God has promised, she is fearful about leaving this life for the next. Among her worries is grieving the loss of her family. In her honesty and humility, Francis voiced a fear common to all humanity.

Throughout her life, religion and spirituality have been important to Frances. She joined the Franciscan Third Order in 1983, was professed in 1985, and has always been a faithful, generous, well-loved member of our fraternity. Until she is welcomed into her heavenly home – and even after - we shall keep her in our prayers and hearts, thanking God for her presence among us.

XI

MARGARET

Some years ago at a day of reflection, Margaret had some quiet time to reflect on her life. She realized that she could go back to when she was four years old and that her spirituality began at that age. Her grandmother always gave her two books to take to church, one on the Blessed Mother, the other about angels.

Margaret remembers looking at the book and admiring the beautiful woman depicted in the pages. She didn't know who she was. Her grandmother had great influence on her spiritual life and the little girl would say prayers at her knee. Above her grandmother's chair hung a Pieta with a sacrament of the sick kit enclosed in its bottom.

At the end of Margaret's bed was a table on which stood a statue of the Sacred Heart. It was therefore not surprising that she developed a devotion to the Sacred Heart during elementary school. She was also enthralled with a huge statue of St. Anthony in the school's entranceway. She thought he must be right up there with St. Joseph because the Baby Jesus sat upon the saint's book. Each year, Margaret studied the catechism in order to win the prize at the end of the school year. The prize was always a statue which joined the other statues on her table with the Sacred Heart.

When she was confirmed at age nine, her grandmother gave her a Book of Saints which included St. Elizabeth of Hungary. She remembers the queen in the book walking down the road, her cape concealing bread intended for the poor. A man, whom Margaret later learned was Elizabeth's brother-in-law, ordered her to open her cloak. When she did, roses spilled out upon the ground. Margaret would later choose this saint as her Franciscan patron.

Years later, while at a supermarket with her sister, a woman came up to Margaret, grabbed her hand, felt the bones in it, and accurately described her personality. She told Margaret that she had the gift of special intuition. She went on to say that somebody named Mary or Ann was watching over her. Margaret's deceased mother's name was Mary. Then the woman told her that she would be widowed in the next ten years. Margaret's sister told her to ignore what she had heard, that she was just an old woman.

In fact, Margaret has not been widowed, but she

does believe in her intuition. Earlier she had dreamt that she was in a tunnel and heard a voice. She answered silently, "You know, God, I don't want to be a nun." Now she believes that if she is widowed early, she would inquire about entering religious life.

On one occasion, Margaret was crossing through the mountains with her husband on the way to Virginia. The fog became so thick that they could barely find their way. They ended up in Maryland where Margaret saw a sign to the shrines of Mary and Elizabeth Ann Seton. Exhausted by the ordeal of the fog, her husband was not interested in going out of his way to see shrines. Heading back to Pennsylvania, he asked a gas attendant for directions. To Margaret's delight, the road took them right to the shrines of the Blessed Mother and Elizabeth Ann Seton. At the shrine of Elizabeth Ann Seton, Margaret noticed several middle-aged women in short habits and carrying attaché cases. She was told at the information office that these women were Sisters of Charity going out to schools and hospitals. She also learned that they have a mother house in Nova Scotia and wondered if she would someday join them.

A few years later, Margaret was teaching catechism in her parish on Monday evenings. She saw a notice in the church bulletin about Secular Franciscans and was disappointed that their Formation meetings were on the same night as her catechism classes. A Secular Franciscan invited Margaret and another interested person to attend the regular meeting which was on a

Wednesday night. They were warmly welcomed by the Fraternity and, to be accommodating, the nights for formation were changed.

During the time of Formation, Margaret had a hard time discerning if she was being called to a Franciscan vocation. She had three priests praying for her because her husband was opposed to it. Finally, Margaret and her husband were able to discuss what was upsetting him. He told her that, knowing it was an Order, and since she had always been spiritual and prayerful, he expected she would be leaving him as soon as she was professed. Being a convert, this frightened him. She reassured him that this had never entered her mind.

At her interview prior to profession, the priest noted that, with her devotion to Saints Anthony and Elizabeth, it was no wonder she had been called to the Secular Franciscan Order. She was professed on March 10, 1991. A friend, who was professed at the same time, decided a year later that it was not her calling after all. Surprised that this could even happen, Margaret became convinced of the extreme importance of prayerful discernment.

When she had been with the fraternity for almost six years, she and her husband moved from the area. Because she was the Formation Director and was instructing two candidates, she stayed on with the fraternity for another two years, driving back and forth. Although she hated to leave the fraternity, coming home late at night from meetings was proving too demanding. Even when the meeting was changed to Sunday afternoons, the two hour drive became unmanageable in winter.

There was a fraternity closer to her new home, but Margaret had a very hard time departing from her own. It had become her family. She wrote about the experience in her journal, describing it as "almost like a death". She read that you should allow yourself sometime between fraternities, and she did this prayerfully.

In the fall, she made the decision to join the closer fraternity. No one there knew she was coming, and she walked in apprehensively. But she needn't have worried. She was welcomed enthusiastically and realized how happy she was to be back with Franciscans.

Sometimes one's faith family has stronger bonds than a physical family, Margaret says. There is definitely grieving by everyone when a member leaves. But because of her welcoming reception at the new fraternity, she believes now that she could go anywhere in the world and be welcomed by Franciscans.

Margaret especially enjoys her present role as a Regional Counselor. She finds it great to work between fraternities, and hears from three of them on a regular basis. She has always believed that the wider Franciscan family should get together.

She has a devout prayer life and tries to cover all forms of prayer – frequent rosaries, adoration once a week, Mass twice a week, and of course, her Office. She follows St. Clare's advice to make work easier by remembering to do everything for God.

She had no intention of moving to her present home in a lovely retirement park, but believes the move was meant to be. She feels that some people are afraid to come into her house because of her many religious articles. The new parish has also been difficult, with some people thinking her overly spiritual.

Margaret doesn't know how she would survive without her fraternity. She takes her Franciscan vocation very seriously and has read that we should live our vocation every day. She conscientiously tries to live her life that way and be a good example to her family.

Margaret states that it's not for us to know our value to others. We have to carry on, doing what we're meant to do, living out our vocation to the best of our ability, while hoping that we're making a difference. She believes in the importance of evangelization. By standing up for our beliefs, we make others examine themselves and question their own actions and lifestyle. Our behaviour influences others, Margaret notes, leading them to come to know Christ.

A family hangs on to spiritual lessons in hard times, she says, and shares the faith. She had an aunt who sent holy cards when she was a child. The girls kept them even though they weren't interested at the time. Her own children gave her a Thomas Kincaid heirloom, a mountain with the resurrected Jesus and the Stations of the Cross.

Margaret loves St. Clare who was blessed with gifts of healing, intuition and compassion. She therefore likes the story relating a mystical experience that transpired one Christmas Eve morning.[11]

XII

JOSEPHINE AND EDWARD

Since God's time is not our time, our life journeys, brief as they are, can be seen as pilgrimages towards the gates of the eternal Eden. Along the way, numerous conversion experiences mark the milestones. Initially, Josephine was unaware of her gradual awakening to a Franciscan vocation. It probably began when she and her husband, Edward, began making annual retreats at a Capuchin retreat house in Michigan. Yet when Edward, encouraged by a Secular Franciscan friend, decided to investigate Franciscan spirituality, Josephine was only mildly supportive.

Still, she couldn't entirely ignore certain positive changes in Edward after he was professed in 1993. He began to regularly attend Mass, receive the Sacraments and become more prayerful. As his values shifted, he developed a subtle peacefulness and acceptance of life's adversities. Five years after her husband's profession into the Order, Josephine entered the inquiry stage of Franciscan formation. Over time, she found in Secular Franciscan spirituality a stirring within her soul at the joy of meeting Jesus in the tradition of Francis and Clare. She also learned the merits and strength of community.

But first, let us go back to the beginning of Josephine's journey. She was born in Montreal where she and her brother were baptized in the Greek Orthodox Church, her father's religion. The family moved to Sudbury, Matawachan and South Porcupine before finally settling in Sarnia. Her father was a plasterer and her hardworking mother walked daily to work at the general hospital. She recalls how her mother was a wonderful baker and cook as well as a religious woman. While her brother married in the Greek Orthodox Church, Josephine has followed the Roman Catholic tradition modeled by her mother.

It was in Sarnia where at age sixteen, Josephine met Edward, who would later become her husband. As a young married couple, they moved to St. Catharines in 1954 so that Edward, a Chief Engineer on ships of the Great Lakes, could more conveniently come home. Nonetheless, he was frequently absent from the family. After the delivery of a stillborn baby, there were three healthy children. It fell to Josephine to raise them mostly alone. It was she who taught them their prayers, took them to church, supervised their various activities, and attended meetings with teachers. Josephine was a determined mother with high expectations for her children.

Their older son enjoyed all sports – hockey, baseball, rowing, and track and field. Their daughter enjoyed swimming and classical guitar. She was involved in ethnic dancing and figure skating, wearing the beautiful costumes painstakingly created by Josephine. The younger son attended cubs and scouts, but preferred books to sports. Nonetheless, his mother made him join a hockey team, insisting that the reluctant coach allow him to participate in hockey practices while avoiding games and tournaments. Josephine notes with amusement that this same son took up hockey at college because he no longer had to compete with his older brother.

Eventually, since Edward wanted a change in work and Josephine was worried about her mother's health, they moved back to Sarnia. Edward, employed as a stationary engineer at Cabot, was finally home all the time. By now, their older son was working, their daughter was at college and their youngest child attended the local Catholic high school.

The couple soon became more involved in parish activities. Josephine was very active in the Catholic Women's League and held various offices in the organization, including that of CWL President. Edward belonged to the Knights of Columbus for many years. Both also embraced the Cursillo movement. It was around then that they began the annual retreats to the Capuchin retreat house. This sparked the interest in Franciscan spirituality that eventually led them to vocations in the Secular Franciscan Order.

A month before Josephine was to be received into the Order, Edward died. Josephine is grateful that her Franciscan family helped her survive that difficult period. She feels blessed that the community has been there to accompany her over other rough spots.

Today she lives in a cozy apartment with her four-year-old Russian Blue cat. She's always had a cat, she says with obvious pleasure. One named Bootsy lived twenty years. Josephine recites the blessings of apartment life. There are no worries about yard work, she feels safe, has underground parking and a close friend who checks up on her.

She shows me the herbs and flowers thriving on her balcony, then leads me back inside to point out treasures on a hall wall. Hanging there are paintings she has done, one with two cats, as well as woodworking pieces carved by Edward. Family pictures are displayed in another room - herself as baby, her uniformed father on horseback in the Russian army, her mother as a young woman. In the dining room is a stained glass cat, her daughter's handiwork.

Josephine opens a closet to reveal the colourfully intricate ethnic costumes she once lovingly sewed for her daughter. She hopes her daughter will take at least one of them as a memento of those past years, a keepsake of a mother's devotion.

Other than having Edward alive, she would not wish for a lifestyle change, she insists. Her younger son, still single, works for an airline and visits her often. Her daughter, working in Ottawa for the department of defense, calls almost every night. Her older son, still crazy about sports, is an executive in steel and is involved with community organizations. He keeps in touch, as do her grandson and two granddaughters, now young adults themselves.

Despite her busy existence, Josephine has lived with a chronic illness for twenty-eight years. Aware that she would die in three or four days without her medication, she simply takes the drugs and refuses to let illness rule her life. Thin and frail, she admits that some days she is "forced to stay home and read". Being a Franciscan helps keep her sound in mind and body, she claims.

Josephine fills many hours with knitting, reading and occasional baking. She enjoys the friendship and monthly socializing with her sister 'Red Hats'. Conceding to less energy than she once had, she exercises twice weekly instead of three times a week. She still belongs to CWL but is minimally active. Daily Mass is no longer possible, but she prays the Office, reads scripture, recites litanies, prays for her family, and petitions God for all who need divine intervention.

For the most part, Josephine spends her time "just feeling relaxed and content," enjoying Franciscan peace. She says that she can relate to the story of unassuming Brother Masseo because, like the friar portrayed here, she's always in the kitchen.[12]

XIII

CHRISTINA

Twenty years ago, Christina wrote joyfully in her journal. "This evening marked the end of my postulancy and the beginning of my novitiate. How happy and excited I felt! I was introduced to our Spiritual Director, a very warm and beautiful priest. Everyone arrived and after Mass, we received the Rite of Admission. We were given the cord of St. Francis and the scapular of the Third Order. How great I felt, filled with love and the Holy Spirit. I'm sure St. Anthony was watching, standing beside St. Francis, smiling and saying, 'Well done, my little one'."

In the ensuing years, living the Gospel Life of a Secular Franciscan has provided Christina with a foundation of peace and acceptance enabling her to survive the losses and illnesses that have beset her. This has been a Godsend because, being conscientious and sensitive, she is, by her own admission, prone to anxiety and worrying.

The story of her life resonates with conversion experiences. She was born in a small coal mining town on Canada's East Coast, the youngest of eight children with five sisters and two brothers. Her mother died when she was two years old. Christina was raised by her father, a coal miner who never remarried, and by her older siblings.

She remembers her father's daily routine. He would come home from work tired, read the paper and join his family for the dinner his children took turns preparing. Before retiring for the night, he would tend his garden, bake bread, or pickle and can his garden produce.

It was left to Christina's sisters to see to it that she made all the Sacraments. She received the Sacraments of Penance and Holy Communion at age six and Confirmation the following year. Her sister dragged the little girl by the hand as they hastened to the church two miles away for Sacramental preparation on Sunday afternoons.

The small, mostly-Catholic community had a single public school. The teachers insisted that their students attend Mass faithfully. Christina was very devoted to God. With a badge of the Sacred Heart pinned to her clothing and a rosary always in her pocket, she recited silent prayers as she walked along.

While recovering from an appendectomy at the age of fourteen, she fell under the spell of the Sisters of St. Martha. She remembers how every noon and evening the nuns went up and down the hospital halls reciting the Angelus and other prayers. She began seeking them out in their office and they, in turn, reached out to her. They expected that she would join their order after she graduated from high school.

However, as graduation approached, Christina longed to become a missionary and began corresponding with the Grey Nuns of the Immaculate Conception. Before she was to enter the convent in September, she left for Sarnia in May to spend the summer there with her sister. Christina, sixteen and enthusiastic, quickly obtained summer employment at an auto parts factory.

Out walking through the neighbourhood with her niece, she frequently passed a variety store. On one occasion, the girls ordered ice cream cones from the store owners' handsome seventeen year old son. The young man gave Christina four scoops which fell off outside the store. A week later, she met him at a wedding shower where he asked her to dance, they laughed about the ice cream incident, and he later walked her home.

The teenagers dated throughout the summer and went to church together every Sunday. Christina bought her new friend a St Christopher medal on a chain which he constantly wore. In August, when she told him about her plans to enter the convent, he tore off the medal and avoided her for a while. After they began meeting again, Christina wrote the convent asking for a year's leave.

Two years later, the young couple married. Christina continued to work until their first child, a daughter, was born. Her husband worked for his family who now owned a pop bottling factory and a milk franchise along with the variety store. When they sold the businesses in order to retire, their son bought out a shoe business with an attached apartment. Christina worked in the store until the first of their two sons were born. The business expanded and the family moved into a new home.

As the children reached school age, they went to the nearby public school rather than the more distant Catholic one. Nonetheless, they attended catechism classes on Saturday mornings and Mass every Sunday.

When the parish priest chastised them for not sending the children to Catholic school, Christina was greatly disturbed. Brought up with "the fear of the Lord", she was still struggling with guilt over her decision to choose marriage over a religious vocation. Despite reassurances from another priest and a nun, she found it difficult to shake the feeling that she had rejected God.

The changes resulting from Vatican II unsettled her further. So now, with her pastor threatening to withhold the Sacraments from her children unless they switched schools, Christina was very upset. For a long time, she walked daily to Mass until the priest relented and welcomed the children into the Sacraments. Christina now points out that her children remain active Catholics unlike some who attended Catholic schools.

Christina first experienced health problems at age fifty. When her children gave her a surprise birthday party in November that year, she felt fatigued. After Christmas, she experienced chest pain and was hospitalized for three weeks. She returned home briefly only to collapse and need to be carried into the emergency department by her husband. She was sent to London where cardiologists found her too sick to undergo an angiogram. Doctors told her husband to take her home and let her die in peace. Because of Christina's anxiety, her family did not inform her of the seriousness of her condition.

She was hospitalized in Sarnia for a while before being sent home. Her husband then set up a hospital bed downstairs so he could care for her. Her younger son took a year off university to help his dad with the family business. When Christine began to show unexpected signs of improvement, she was again sent to London for an angiogram. After much prayer, she opted for triple bypass surgery which, by the grace of God, she survived.

Two years later, she and her husband went to Portugal for a holiday. While praying at Fatima, they both saw Mary at the same time and were moved to joyful tears. Christina believes that this was another conversion experience preparing them for difficulties still to come.

Christina later went to a 'Life in the Spirit' seminar,

becoming so alive that she felt she could walk on air. After being slain in the spirit, she went home and asked her husband if she looked different. He told her that said she was "red all over". This conversion experience prompted her to search for deeper spirituality. She encouraged her husband to make a Cursillo weekend retreat so that she could follow suit.

Christina recalls that on her Cursillo weekend she hoped to go to the St. Theresa table but was assigned instead to the St. Francis of Assisi table. She came off the weekend highly motivated, attended ultreyas, joined small groups and asked to read at ultreya Masses. Her enthusiasm extended into her parish where she wanted to become a reader but couldn't because she already belonged to the choir.

Christina was very disappointed not to be asked to join the team preparing for the next Cursillo. She was miffed to see the team attend weekday evening Mass as a group on their meeting nights. After that she refused to be on team even when invited.

One evening following Mass, Christina saw a different group of people participating in an Initiation Rite at the altar. She was very moved by the experience and says she "felt so with the Lord... like the Spirit had hit her... like a veil was lifted."

One of the people participating in the mysterious Rite belonged to the parish 'Caring and Sharing' ministry with Christine. She pressed the woman to tell her about Franciscanism and Christine was filled with questions. How does one live the Gospel life? What does 'Gospel to life' and 'life to Gospel' mean? She wanted to join right away and waited impatiently for the next Formation class to begin. As soon as she became a Candidate in the Secular Franciscan Order, it became clear to her why she had not become more involved in Cursillo. She was home with her new Secular Franciscan family.

We dwell in the valley of tears and, while being Franciscan cannot shield us from the death of loved ones, it can give us strength. Christina's son-in-law, a physician, died six weeks after being diagnosed with cancer. Although not Catholic, he regularly attended church with his family and received Viaticum before he expired. With her fatherless sons aged fifteen, thirteen and seven, Christina's daughter returned to Sarnia to be near her family. Christina was able to provide spiritual and physical support to her grieving daughter who, in time, resumed her nursing career.

A few years later, tragedy struck again. Her daughter also fell victim to a cancer which all too quickly advanced to a terminal state. Christina recalls how she and her husband would go to the Adoration Chapel and beg Jesus to cure their daughter. She also remembers standing in church before the crucifix reflecting on Mary having to endure the crucifixion and death of her beloved son.

A few days before she slipped into a coma, Christina's daughter sat up in bed and said, "Mom, Father Solanus is standing at the foot of my bed." She described the Franciscan friar to Christina who, although she could not herself see him, agreed that he was there.

As her daughter lay dying in her arms, Christina told her "Go to Jesus now. He's right there waiting for you, and so is John."

Christina was devastated at losing her only daughter. She believes that she was able to bear her terrible loss because, while she was grieving, she belonged to a Franciscan community and was sustained by the prayers of the community.

She continues to struggle with her cross of anxiety and worry. Two years ago, she was justifiably alarmed when her husband had a serious heart attack and underwent triple bypass surgery. To her immense relief, he continues to do well. More recently, a grandson was confronted with a life-threatening illness. Christina instructed the young man to pray before the crucifix saying, I give you myself wholly and totally but do with me what you will. "But expect to be healed," she assured him. She is confident that he will be fine.

Since her earlier heart surgery, Christina had a partial thyroidectomy. After enduring twenty-one anxious days following a recent biopsy, she was pronounced fine but must now have yearly ultrasounds and biopsies. A few months ago, sent to hospital with generalized pain and edema, she was diagnosed with severe chronic anaemia. Since then, despite medication, Christina remains fatigued and pale.

She finds she has to push herself to do things these days. She's always been involved with the Catholic Women's League and belongs to a choir which sings at parish funerals. Her husband serves at these same Funeral Masses with the Knights of Columbus. "There are so many funerals," she observes. She notes regretfully the increasing responsibilities placed on the shoulders of elderly parishioners. Young parents sending their children to Catholic schools are not willing to participate in parish ministries. Many do not attend church or contribute financially to their parishes.

But for Christina, being a Franciscan has given her true happiness. She feels that in growing spiritually, she is continuously developing greater acceptance of her trials and deeper appreciation of her many blessings. She perceives the languor she experiences prior to church services or Franciscan gatherings as the physical consequences of aging and failing health rather than spiritual apathy.

She can relate to St. Clare who on her deathbed reassured Brother Rainaldo with the words, "After I once came to know the grace of my Lord Jesus Christ through his servant Francis, no pain has been bothersome, no penance too severe, no weakness, dearly beloved brother, has been hard."

At the luncheon following her daughter's funeral on December 23, Christina's family had the poem, "My First Christmas in Heaven," read aloud. Drawing upon this hope-filled memory, Christina appreciates the story of St. Francis' first re-enactment of the Christmas manger scene at Greccio.[13]

AFTERWARD

*P*raised be God, the Father of our Lord Jesus Christ, the Father of mercies, and the God of all consolations! He comforts us in our afflictions and thus enables us to comfort those who are in trouble, with the same consolation we have received from him. As we have shared much in the suffering of Christ, so through Christ do we share abundantly in his consolation. These words from the second letter of Paul to the Corinthian community speak to Christians in all communities.

Listening to the stories of my Secular Franciscan brothers and sisters has enabled me to see them in an enhanced manner. It has also given me a deeper appreciation of the Communion of Saints. I see the members of my fraternity as belonging to the Church Militant, fighting on the side of good. In a world where injustice and selfishness thrive, these Franciscans instill love, compassion and hope.

Although they appear to be ordinary citizens of the

world with everyday limitations, weakness and failings, they are illuminated with God's graces. I often find myself in awe of their humility, simplicity, generosity and serenity.

Still, lest I canonize them before their time, I must point out that they can sometimes be querulous, fretful and annoying. They are, after all, a community of humans.

And it is through this human frailty that that we inspire one another. It is in our weakness that we exude strength. It is in our daily struggle to live the Gospel Life that we model the peace and joy associated with Saints Francis and Clare.

My Franciscan brothers and sisters nurture my own calling. They regularly remind me that my vocation as a Secular Franciscan is integral to who I am. Because of my Franciscan community, I see my life as a ministry and my writing as a mission. Novels and scriptural commentaries alike become vehicles to embrace environmental issues, promote social justice and defend the Faith.

In *The Road Trip: Life With Autism*, co-authored with my son, Kevin, I related my Franciscan journey within the context of family dynamics. There is no need for me to retell my story here. The stories of my fraternity sisters and brothers aptly present the heart and soul of Franciscan spirituality. Francis of Assisi provided the model and encouragement to seek joy, peace and beauty amidst the trials of the world.

It was always the supreme and particular desire of blessed

Francis to possess an abiding joy of spirit outside times of prayer and Divine Office. This was the virtue that he especially loved to see in his brethren, and he often reproached them when they showed signs of gloom and despondency.

He used to say, 'If the servant of God strives to obtain and preserve both outwardly and inwardly the joyful spirit which springs from purity of heart and is acquired through devout prayer, the devils have no power to hurt him, and say, "We can find no way to get at him or hurt him, because this servant of God preserves his joy both in trouble and in prosperity." But the devils are delighted when they discover means to quench or disturb the devotion and joy which springs from true prayer and other holy practices. For if the devil can obtain a hold over one of God's servants, he will soon transform a single hair into a log to hurl at him unless he is a wise man and takes care to remove and destroy it as quickly as possible by the power of holy prayer, contrition and satisfaction.

Therefore, my brothers, since this spiritual joy springs from cleanness of heart and the purity of constant prayer, it must be your first concern to acquire and preserve these two virtues, so as to possess this inward joy that I so greatly desire and love to see both in you and myself, and which edify our neighbour and reproach our enemy. For it is the lot of the Devil and his minions to be sorrowful, but ours always to be happy and rejoice in the Lord.' [14]

Although we may be outside Eden's gates, all creation rightly gives thanks for God's joy and peace. This is proclaimed in both the New Testament and within the Hebrew Scriptures. *The hills are girded with joy, the meadows covered with flocks, the valleys are decked with wheat*, sings the psalmist. *They shout for joy, yes, they sing.*[15]

St. Paul assures us that *the peace of God which surpasses all understanding, will guard your hearts and your minds in Christ Jesus.*[16]

In the letter of James we read, *Whenever you face trials of any kind, consider it nothing but joy, because you know that the testing of your faith produces endurance.*[17] James tells us to welcome temptations and trials as a means to endurance, which, in turn, makes us mature and complete. God readily grants us wisdom to deal with the ordeals of life if we but ask.

When God sent Adam and Eve forth from the garden, they were still surrounded by the beauty of creation and were, as well, entrusted with its care. Outside the gates of Eden, we too have the responsibility to carry out this trust.

As they go through the Bitter Valley they make it a place of springs; the early rain covers it with blessings. They go from strength to strength.[18] Prevented from entering the garden by cherubim and a flaming sword, we nonetheless have been given the power to build bridges, right wrongs and light the way for others. Confidently bearing the highways to Zion in our hearts, we walk through the valleys with ever growing strength.

FOOTNOTES

1. *Mirror of Perfection*, 27
2. *Legend of the Three Companions*, VI, 16-19
3. *Legend of the Three Companions*, 48 -51 and *Bonaventure Major Life*, III, 10
4. *Legend of the Three Companions*, VI, 19-20
5. *Little Flowers of St. Francis*, VIII
6. *Little Flowers of St. Francis*, XXI

   In an earlier text than the one cited here, Bartholomew of Pisa testified in his Conformities, that on Mount Alverna, St. Francis once converted a fierce bandit. Local tradition adds that he was called Lupo (wolf) because of his savage cruelty, but that the Saint renamed him Agnello (lamb). He is reported to have become a holy friar.

7. **See Appendix I**, Day 14
8. *Celano, Second Life*, CL, 198;

Francis and Clare: The Complete Works, page 149;

Admonitions, 27,

Omnibus, 86

9. *Francis and Clare: The Complete Works*, pages 104 – 106

10. *Little Flowers of St. Francis*, XVI

11. *Little Flowers of St. Francis*, XXXV

12. *Flowers of St. Francis*, XII

13. *Celano, First Life*, XXX, 84-85

14. *Mirror of Perfection*, 95

15. *Psalm 65*:12-13

16. *Philippians* 4:7

17. *James* 1:2-3

18. *Psalm 84*:6-7

APPENDIX
Original Notes and Readings
For Pilgrimage To Assisi

Day 1
Itinerary

An evening flight leaving Toronto's Pearson Airport and arriving at Rome's Fumicino Airport. Be certain to arrive at the airport early and be prepared for our friends in security and customs!

Pilgrimage Notes

Pilgrimage begins with an expectancy of the heart, a longing of the soul. My pilgrim companions and I are seeking conversion to a deeper state of grace. Four of the pilgrims, Jim, Anna, Virginia and Brother Alan, have agreed to share their journals.

At Pearson Airport, we mill about, greeting fellow pilgrims as they arrive singly and in small groups. Most of them belong to Brother Alan's St. Felix of

Calibrini Fraternity, and Jim and I are grateful to have been included. Brother Alan presents each of us with a manila envelope containing Morning and Evening Prayer along with booklets containing readings from Franciscan biographies and contemporary writers. He's an historian and has compiled an impressive amount of material for each day.

Because of the long waits now imposed on international travellers, we wander about, read, sit and fidget. We have not yet fully extracted ourselves from the people, events and stresses of daily life. Outwardly subdued, we carry secret hopes and inner excitement.

I have packed lightly but have included an empty nylon bag to hold potential gifts and keepsakes, a rather touristy distraction to my spiritual quest. In my carry-on bag I have petitions to Saints Francis and Clare from our own fraternity, St. Anthony of Padua in Sarnia. Being in possession of these hand written prayers and pleas seems to enhance the importance of my journey. At the same time, I am humbled by the openness and trust of my Secular Franciscan sisters and brothers, and moved by their faith and sincerity.

Jim: I feel much at peace in anticipation of the trip. It's been quite hectic preparing, what with Mother's death and getting the house ready to drywall. But I have felt quite peaceful all week. I hope that this pilgrimage deepens that peace and that it stays with me.

Anna: I hope to satisfy my quest to find what my

heart needs to experience.

Virginia: I am going on this pilgrimage to come back renewed in spirit, and to meet Jesus in a special way like St. Francis did.

Brother Alan: I am going with the hope of not only developing a pilgrimage ministry, but also and more importantly, to share Francis, Clare and Assisi with my pilgrims on a more personal level.

Franciscan Readings

How an abbot felt the power of Francis' prayer - *Celano, Second Life*, LXVII, 101

The knowledge and the memory of St. Francis - *Celano, Second Life*, LXVIII, 102

St. Francis and the Doctor of the Order of Preachers - *Mirror of Perfection*, 53

St. Clare on the interior life - *First Letter of Clare to Blessed Agnes of Prague*

Day 2
Itinerary

Arrival in Rome mid-morning, boarding a private coach to our accommodations at Casa Il Rosario. Unpack, acclimatize to our new surroundings and time zone, rest. Gathering orientation, presentation of tomorrow's activities and common prayer.

Pilgrimage Notes

The flight was essentially uneventful with some pleasantries, such as the food, and only an occasional episode of near panic. One of these occurred when I awoke from a period of sleep and wondered where I was. With my eyes still closed, I realized I was not on terra firma, and became terrified. I prayed until I felt I could open my eyes without setting off mass hysteria among my airborne companions.

Milan at last! After another flight to Rome's Fumicino Airport, a small bus delivers us from Rome Airport to our accommodations at Casa Il Rosario. In between each flight and coach, Brother Alan obsessively counts to fourteen over and over. He reminds me of a mother hen clucking over its brood, but David comments that it's like herding cats. David's description is probably more accurate, since Alan's group is not nearly as compliant as chicks!

Amazingly we arrive in one piece and all accounted for at Il Rosario. Nestled in the heart of ancient Rome, this convent is *a house of welcome for pilgrims and tourists*. To locate it, one must walk along the narrow Via Sant' Agata dei Goti, and there, behind one of many doorways, is the villa. The rooms, small and simple, overlook the street (as ours did) or a cozy inner courtyard. There is a private chapel, a roof terrace and a dining lounge. The sisters, who speak little English, are gracious and friendly.

Today's weather is a mix of sun and clouds with on and off rain. Although it's early afternoon, we head exhausted to our rooms to shower and sleep. In the evening, Jim and I wander the streets of Rome, passing near the night-lit Coliseum. We have a leisurely meal in a pleasant Italian sidewalk restaurant.

Has it been a spiritual day? Do I feel yet like I'm really on pilgrimage? In truth, I feel physically and mentally exhausted, rather ill, and spiritually lethargic. In consideration of his pilgrims' obvious fatigue, Brother Alan tells us to do Evening Prayer alone or in groups as we wish. Jim and I pray together and feel somewhat renewed.

Brother Alan: After a long day of travel, a delay in leaving Milan, and a subsequent delay in connecting with our coach driver at the Rome airport, we make all our connections. Tired yet joyful, we arrive at our accommodations, Il Rosario in Rome. After settling in we decide to look for some food, realizing soon that almost everything is closed. After some walking around we happen upon an open café. By this time we are suffering from hunger, sore legs and tired feet only to have sandwiches and drinks. People are grumbling and I feel very doubtful and insecure as the leader. Feeling somewhat refreshed after eating, our group heads off for some sight-seeing. I go with Bette Ann and Virginia. We walk over the Capitoline Hill and cross the Testevere River. There we find our goals: an ancient ruined Roman Bridge and an Etruscan sewer, predating the Roman republic.

Bette Ann provides us with an excellent historical commentary and I can safely vent my frustration and self-doubts to my friends. We enjoy a light dinner across from the Forum and return for a good night's rest, something I think we all need.

Franciscan Readings

St. Francis and Ecology - *Celano, Second Life*, CXXVI, 167, CXXVII,168, CXXIX,170
On his love for water, rocks, wood and flowers - *Mirror of Perfection*, 118
St. Clare and contemplation - *Second Letter of Clare to Blessed Agnes of Prague*

Day 3

Itinerary

Morning Prayer. Time to explore Rome, individual and small group explorations. Possible sites which are close by: the Roman Forum, the Coliseum, the Vatican, the Spanish Steps, the Church of the Immaculate Conception (Capuchin), Trevi Fountain, Emmanuale Vittorio Fountain. (Pick carefully as our time is limited!)

Pilgrimage Notes

The streets of Rome are wet in the morning sun. Brother Alan has advised us to tour the city in small groups. So Anna, Jim and I set off together, armed with umbrellas against the threat of scattered showers.

We will begin at the Vatican, which the three of us have seen previously, and then we will visit St. John Lateran, a new experience.

In the Piazza San Pietro, we fall in line with other pilgrims and tourists waiting to go through security checks. Something new since last year's September 11. Then we spot Brother Alan's group and wander over to greet them. Alan has found a tour guide, Cathy from Boston, and invites us to join them. Cathy proves to be very helpful. She stresses the massive size of everything in St. Peter's, and points out lines on the floor which mark out the measurements of huge-but–still-smaller other churches. We see Michelangelo's moving Pieta carved when the artist was but twenty-four years old. For the first time, I become aware that the basilica is filled, not with paintings, but with mosaics!

St. Peter's is beautiful beyond description – awesome even the second time around. Somehow, though, I am not moved beyond a normal tourist's emotion. But all that will change in the afternoon when we enter the Lateran. Along the way to the ancient cathedral, we stop to admire St. Mary Major, largest of the numerous Roman churches dedicated to the Madonna. It has beautiful, ancient artwork and a marvelous ceiling of ornately carved, gilded wood.

And now the moment our Franciscan hearts were unknowingly waiting for: St. John Lateran, "Mother and first of all Churches in the World." Popes resided here from 324 to 1305, and it remains the Pope's cathedral of Rome. Five Ecumenical Councils took place here and many Diocesan Synods. Here it was that in 1209 Francis of Assisi received approval of his Rule of Life from Pope Innocent III.

The three of us pray and wander blissfully here for much of the afternoon. Intermittent pouring rain outside and loud claps of thunder seem to add to the atmosphere. I am enchanted with the lovely, 13th century cloister, peaceful in rain showers. I take in the modern windows above the cloister, trying to imagine how peaceful it might be for those friars who live here yet. I gaze in awe upon the huge marble statues of apostles, paintings of patriarchs, green marble columns, wonderful frescoes.

Jim is struck by the words carved on one of the Lateran's five front doors, "A pilgrimage is a path of conversion, an interior preparation for a renewal of the heart". I am impressed that Jim is able to carry on so calmly. Earlier in the afternoon he had his wallet stolen as we rode the infamous Rome bus 40. Although his wallet contained his driver's license, health card, assorted papers, one credit card and some cash, most of his valuables were in a money belt. We were able to phone in a cancellation on his credit card. And thankfully, our passports were safely at Il Rosario.

Anna: I found St. Peter's Basilica interesting, but too imposing. However, at St. John Lateran, I felt at home, peaceful, and in the presence of Francis and my roots. I will return here when we return to Rome.

Brother Alan's Journal: Today Margaret, Beatrice, Simone, Marcel and I are off to visit the Vatican by taxi. Upon our arrival we are fortunate to meet up with Cathy, a wonderful person from Boston, who has offered us a tour which we accept. Before we begin the guided tour, a part of our group who has taken Roma transit also happens upon us! What luck: we all get to share in the experience of her tour which was quite excellent! Her knowledge of the artists, architects and sculpture was rich and deep.

After visiting the tombs of the popes, I go to explore the possibilities of touring the "Scavi". As I passed the gate I heard a loud click of heels, only to realize that the guards had snapped to attention! How embarrassing, little me in the expanse of that arch, and guards coming to attention (the power of a religious habit made manifest!!!). It somehow doesn't seem congruent with being a Franciscan and Capuchin...

After an excellent lunch at a charming Trattoria, we tour the Vatican Museum and the Sistine Chapel. I am so happy how Margaret is in awe of the Sistine Chapel and in particular Michelangelo's "Creation". When we left it was raining hard but we endured and made our way back to our meeting place at the Vatican... Only Beatrice and Marcel are not there!

We revisit the Trattoria but they aren't there either. With a sense of panic setting in, we return to the Tomb of the Popes so we can get to the fountain outside the exit, but to no avail. We spend some time under Bornini's colonnade, sheltered from the rains. Before we decide to return to Il Rosario ourselves, Simone goes back alone.

What a surprise! The spirit is truly working…both Marcel and Beatrice are waiting for a taxi as we arrive…the lost are found (from either perspective)!

Franciscan Readings
Francis and Pope at St. John Lateran -
Legend of the Three Companions, 48 -51
Pope approves rule and confers tonsures -
Bonaventure Major Life, III, 10
St. Clare on Jesus, the mirror of eternity -
Third Letter of Clare to Blessed Agnes of Prague

Day 4
Itinerary
Travel by private coach to Assisi arriving at St. Anthony's Guesthouse. Unpack and settle in…we will be here for the next 10 days! Welcoming introduction to Assisi plus a brief walking tour to locate key sites, (i.e.: Piazza del Commune, the Temple of Minerva, Basilica of St. Francis, Basilica of St. Clare, San Ruffino, etc., and situate ourselves in Francis and

Clare's presence. Evening Prayer.

Pilgrimage Notes

The highway to Assisi leaves the cobblestones of Rome to wind through a green countryside, hills, vineyards and orchards. As the bus travels the autostrada toward our destination, the sunny day becomes gradually hazy. I have been feeling unwell since arriving in Italy. I find it harder to be contemplative and realize that people who are ill must experience life through a veil of pain or dullness. Yet Francis and Clare were able to use physical ills and pain to purify the flesh and heighten the spiritual.

As we ride along, roadside signs point to places we associate with Francis: Terni, Spolito, Foligno, Perugia. Everywhere there are hills, hills, hills. And on these hills are houses, sheep, trees, churches, castles, buildings of stucco, brick and stone. Finally a sign catches everyone's attention: Assisi 23! The pilgrims chat happily with subdued excitement.

Assisi seems to inspire the poetic nature of all who enter its welcoming walls, and has been praised variously. Its titles include *holy city, enchanted city, temple, house of prayer, holy reliquary, citadel of the spirit, city of light, heavenly cloister, garden of peace and bliss, home of dreams and serenity, fountain of grace, cascade of blessings.* We are staying at St. Anthony's Guest House, operated by the Franciscan Sisters of the Atonement. Jim and I stayed here six years ago with one of our sons, and are happy to recognize Sister Susan, a most accommodating host. The guesthouse is charming and conveniently situated between St. Clare's Basilica and St. Rufino's Cathedral.

The view from our room takes my breath away. Tiered private gardens drop downward to the piazza of Santa Chiara. And there is the lovely stone basilica itself, reaching heavenward in artful simplicity. A slight movement in the adjacent garden below catches my eye: a lizard peers about from a flower pot. Then it steps out, walks casually across a stone path, and climbs a tree to the higher courtyard right below our window.

In the evening we follow Brother Alan through the streets of Assisi. Although we are delighted to again be in this wonderful city, both Jim and I are slightly under the weather and find it hard to keep up. Some of our more senior pilgrims are also struggling with the steep incline of the cobbled streets. The day ends with Evening Prayer and sharing.

Jim: We are leaving for Assisi now. Yesterday's churches were very uplifting. How dedicated to God the people were to create all the magnificent paintings, sculptures, mosaics, columns, stonework and decorative flooring.

Virginia: The first day in Assisi made me feel connected with St. Francis. Walking where St. Francis walked for his entire life made me focus on him and on what his example did for the people of Assisi.

Brother Alan: As we travel north, the beauty of the regions and the distant Appenine Mountains are a soothing effect on our spirits from the rush of Rome. As we near Assisi, road signs with familiar names like Foligno, Spello, Spoleto and Perugia inspire excited conversations among the group. For myself I feel as if I'm coming to a second Rome. I begin to recall stories of Francis associated with those places and feel an embrace of awe and familiarity. I am so excited and happy to share Assisi with my friends.

After the evening meal, we do a walking orientation of Assisi. I fear this may have been a bad decision on my part. Some of our seniors I know are struggling with the streets and slopes of Assisi. I will have to apologize at prayer tonight and remind myself to ensure a slower pace now as much as we can and yet indulge what Assisi has to offer our spirits. God, please help me to make right and compassionate decisions...

A wonderful evening prayer! I am in awe of the capacity for prayer that was shown tonight. If it lasts the remainder of our pilgrimage, and I'm sure it will, all will be well. The group doesn't know it but we will also have guests on our day trips, an Atonement sister and possibly Brother John Juhl.

Franciscan Readings
Young Francis of Assisi -

Legend of the Three Companions, 7 – 8
Francis after his conversion-
Legend of the Three Companions, 21
Clare and the three dimensions of the mirror -
Fourth Letter of Clare to Blessed Agnes of Prague

Day 5

Itinerary

Morning Prayer and recollection of Francis' early life – the beginnings of our 10 day conversation with Francis and Clare of Assisi. We will visit Chiesa Nuova, San Ruffino (the baptismal place of Francis and Clare), the Piazza in front of San Ruffino which borders on Clare's childhood home, the Piazza of Mary Major and the Bishop's residence. In the evening we will recall the stories of Greccio, Fonte Columbo and Poggio Bustone.

Pilgrimage Notes

Jim awakens with severe back pain, probably from helping carry the luggage of the older pilgrims. For my part, I've had abdominal pain and nausea since arriving in Italy. Nonetheless, we are both determined that we will not permit health concerns to ruin our pilgrimage. So…Jim wears my back brace, and I try to eliminate wheat and dairy products (nearly impossible in Italy!) from my diet.

Following on the heels of Brother Alan, we tour

Assisi. In front of San Rufino, Alan tells us stories associated with the cathedral. Francis and Clare were both baptized here, the bishop presented Clare with a palm branch here on Palm Sunday, and Francis meditated in the side chapel. Inside San Ruffino, Jim lights a candle for his Mother. On the side wall of the piazza is the site of Clare's apartment.

Chiesa Nuova is thought to be built over the birthplace and home of Francis and the family shop. Here Francis was incarcerated by his father for his erratic behaviour and later freed by his mother. We stop by the tiny Oratory of San Francesco Piccolino where legend says Pica gave birth to Francis.

We visit Santa Maria Maggiore and the adjacent Piazza Vescovado where the bishop lived and where Francis took off his clothing and stood naked. We stand beneath umbrellas admiring a plain stone building which Alan said had been the Church of St. Gregory where Francis felt called to be knight. And directly across the street was Bernard of Quintavalle's house.

There is a Youth Festival in Assisi every year at this time. Thus we are treated to singing and instrumental music in the afternoons and evenings. The revelry stops around 11:00 p.m. Nonetheless, cars and people seem non-intrusive as we pilgrims trudge along the streets behind Brother Alan.

A pilgrimage is a condensed version of life's journey, convoluted and evolving. It is an ongoing struggle to remain committed to conversion. Always there exists tension between community and privacy, social action and contemplation. We are all impressed with the dedication of Brother Alan, his enthusiasm, and his concern for our well-being. He is also an historian with a wealth of Franciscan information. Earlier today, for example, he told us that it is now commonly felt that Francis died of leprosy.

Night Prayer assures me that I am indeed in the company of pilgrims. Brother Alan gives us an overview of tomorrow's agenda and we retire for the night.

Jim: Morning Prayer was enjoyable and specific to Assisi. Brother Alan deserves a lot of credit for his superb preparation. Despite my back, I feel quite at peace and happy to be here.

Virginia: At Piazza Vescovado St. Francis left everything and gave himself to God without asking 'What will I do tomorrow for food or clothing?' Instead he emptied himself and trusted the Lord. I am a professed member of the Secular Franciscan Order, but today the place where Francis stripped became real for me.

Brother Alan: My heart sinks as I awake. It is still raining out…it began last night. I was hoping we would arise to an Assisi dawn full of sunlight. Yet I somehow sense that this group may opt from visiting today's sites in the rain. The bells of Santa Chiara and Santa Maria degli Angeli toll in the mists as if answering each other. I am still embraced with a sense of peace and trust... this is truly Holy Ground, as tangible now as during my first visit in 1999. God! How I love this place.

We enjoy another beautiful morning prayer and I offer some historical and spiritual input regarding the places we are about to spend time at today. San Ruffino touches Margaret... I will be interested to learn just how. Chiesa Nuova we explore as one of the places where our saint and brother Francis lived... my personal skepticism prevents me from believing that this is the location. Particularly so when I recall the very moving experience I had in the upper room of the former English speaking pilgrim centre which I believe is the home of Francis.

We finish up at Santa Maria Maggiore and the Piazza Vescovado where Francis stripped himself and renounce his father and his family's wealth. The frescoes inside are ancient and beautiful. The older in Byzantine style were probably viewed by Francis! The thought of that and sharing the same sight is awe inspiring.

Before we break up for lunch I take them to a small street corner and present St. Gregorio to them. Then asking who can tell me the name of the first brother to follow Francis, I explain that just behind them is the former home of Bernard of Quintavalle. The reaction is excited and leaves me fulfilled in that I have managed to include such a pleasant surprise! Tonight we gather for evening prayer and sharing. I can't wait to hear how today has affected everyone!

Again tonight prayer was deep running and meaningful. Our sharing has been inspirational for each of us. I am left feeling indebted toward each pilgrim for their presence and growth as shared. I am also feeling very fulfilled regarding the reception and participation on the part of each. I feel now that I can indeed successfully lead a pilgrimage, and for me this confirms my discernment and direction for a possible future ministry.

Franciscan Readings
Bernardo di Quintavalle's house -
Legend of the Three Companions, 27 – 28
The cure of the stricken oxen -
Legend of Perugia, 57
The cure of the ailing cleric -
Legend of Perugia, 58

Day 6
Itinerary
Road Trip! By private coach we will visit the Rieti Valley – and the significant Franciscan sites of Greccio, Fonte Columbo and Poggio Bustone. We will celebrate Francis' Christmas Crèche in prayer at Greccio and visit the monastery built by St. Bonaventure at the site.

Pilgrimage Notes

We are travelling to the Rieti valley to visit Greccio, Fonte Colombo and Poggio Bustone, places dear to Francis and his companions. Today I feel called to pray specifically for conversion and a heightened awareness of my sins. Through our bus window, I absorb the exotic Italian countryside. We pass industrial buildings, vineyards, olive orchards, small farms, chickens, sheep, ever-charming medieval hill top towns, an ancient friary. The houses, high and isolated, are plain and shuttered on the outside. They are two and three-storied with lots of stairs. Trees, like at home, are both evergreen and deciduous. But here palm trees grow alongside pines. On the Autostrada del Sole, cars pass between trucks and buses – even around curves – using the centre line as third lane! Initially startled, I soon realize this is a normal driving technique.

At Greccio, the Franciscan Bethlehem, we visit St. Bonaventure's dormitory and St. Francis' cell. In the chapel, Brother Alan tells us a story about the ivory bambino carved by Luigi for his blind daughter. Several pilgrim strangers including some nuns, listen on. Also at Greccio is a portrait of an ailing Francis wiping his ailing eye. It was at Fonte Columbo, the fountain of doves, that Francis put together his final Rule of Life in 1223, and had his eyes cauterized. In the Chapel of the Magdelene, where Francis painted a tau at a window, we renewed our commitment to Franciscan life and reflected on the Gospel Life. It is necessary to deepen our discernment and permit our vows to evolve and develop.

Poggio Bustone is high, rugged and impressive. Early in his ministry, Francis and six companions came upon a deserted hermitage here. In a cave, Francis confesses faults and asks to be shown his sins. Two or three friars live in this starkly beautiful place today.

The day ends with prayer and sharing in the guesthouse chapel. I am filled with thanksgiving – for the privilege of being in this sacred place, for the gifts of Francis and Clare, for Brother Alan, for my fellow pilgrims.

Jim: The manger scenes at Greccio are exotic and priceless. Creating the first crèche, a major influence of Francis, is not as widely known as his love of animals and appreciation of creation. But the manger scene is most important and has spread throughout the world. Greccio demonstrates this. The most moving part of the day for me was the renewal of our Franciscan vows at Fonte Columbo. We renewed them in the same place that Francis wrote The Rule. Wow! Secular Franciscans worldwide would give anything to do that. And we did it! I'm amazed that Francis would travel so far through such difficult terrain to find a place of rest.

Virginia: The painting of Francis impressed me most in this day. That picture spoke to me about simplicity and humility, and Francis preached to me without words as he said. That suffering for his brothers and sisters made clear to me how he imitated Jesus. By his suffering and example, Francis built community, peace, love and fraternity. When I reflected upon this, I realized that I am nothing before God compared to Francis. It became clear to me that I have to look deep inside me. Am I really a changed person following Christ as I should? Do I give example to others? Am I really living a Gospel life? This made me reflect on what I must change and what I must continue in order to improve. I felt a great joy and inner peace renewing our promises at Fonte Columbo, the place where St. Francis wrote The Rule. This day was so special for me.

Brother Alan: Rieti! Last night I was praying that the day would arrive with a sunny disposition, yet as we left Assisi the clouds, although broken, hung low and heavy. The drive to Greccio, our first stop, was long and at times, wet. Our driver, Quinto, and Virginia, who was born near here, described for us many of the towns and sites along our route. Our arrival was welcome, we were hungry and needed a rest. But as I feared, it was raining. Nonetheless, we persevere and climbing the wide steps of stone, enter the chapel commemorating Francis' institution of the Christmas Crèche.

I have chosen to read the well-worn story of Luigi and Francis and am aware of more people moving around us. Another group has joined us as I read the story! As I look up I am greeted with many faces, most seeming to be lost in the story and the significance of the place.

We explore the old cells built by Bonaventure, spend time in the ancient chair, and learn of a new image of Francis. We afterwards enjoy our bag lunches while at Greccio for, as we exit, we discover that the rain has stopped, the sun is out and the air is warming up. The beautiful vistas across the Rieti are plainly seen. We are all amazed and enthralled by the beauty before us. Many begin to understand and to re-define Francis' joy at creation.

Our second stop takes us to Fontecolombo where we look around. The sacred cave and fountain spring are below us at the base of a steep walk. Although I would love for them to see these things, there is time to consider and the difficult walk back up!

Moving to the Chapel of the Magdelene we sing, we pray and we renew our Franciscan Commitments after having listened to reading, comparing the nuances of how Francis' rule evolved. I think this was probably the most moving and poignant moment of today: Re-committing in the very place where the Franciscan Rule sprang into life! Afterwards we visited Francis' Dormitory where he lived while here, and where his eye cauterization took place.

Taking leave of Fonte Columbo, we journeyed

across the valley to Poggio Bustone where we feasted on the panorama spread out before us. From the monastery church of San Giancomo, the entire Rieti Valley lay exposed before us! Again God provided a lift to the clouds as sunshine streams across the valley.

We speak of and reflect upon reconciliation, Francis' and our own lived experiences. Then we embark on our bus and slowly descend through the town site below the monastery, and make our way home. Assisi, as we draw closer, is shrouded in clouds and rain…as if we have been missed during our first day trip. Tonight prayer, singing and sharing… I can hardly wait to hear from my brothers and sisters.

I was deeply heartened when two or three spoke very positively about the experience and content. My dreams for this are coming true beyond my expectations… Through this their hearts are growing new and deeper Franciscan roots! God is indeed a benevolent God.

Franciscan Readings
The manger at Greccio -
Celano, First Life, XXX, 84-85
Third Order fraternity at Greccio -
Legend of Perugia, 34
Confirming the Rule -
Bonaventure Major Life, IV 11

Day 7

Itinerary

Morning Prayer. Today is a "Free Day". You may wish to visit Perugia, Spoleto, the Church at Rivo Torto, the Rocca Majiore, the Carceri, the Church of San Stephano, or the Assisi cemetery where some noteworthy Franciscan friars are buried.

Pilgrimage Notes

Although today was designated as a 'Free day', Brother Alan has presented us with the option of visiting the Carceri. Of course we choose this, and so, after Morning Prayer we happily depart. The Carceri is situated on Mount Subasio about four kilometres outside Assisi. In this secluded place, Francis and his friars prayed and dwelt in caves, huts and the surrounding woods. One of these caves became a chapel to which is attached a small hermitage.

Francis appealed to Sylvester and Clare to help him choose between prayer and preaching. His life thereafter became one of itinerant preacher strengthened with periods of solitary prayer. He was both mendicant and contemplative. Francis established twenty-one hermitages and wrote a Rule of Life for Hermitages.

A regular rhythm of solitude gives serenity, humility, simplicity and depth to our lives. We need to let go of our comfortable devotions, advises Brother Alan, and practice meditation in order to really hear

God. This morning, at meditation before Morning Prayer, I try to focus: Lord help me… help me…help me over and over. I am feeling a struggle, trying too hard. Then I switch to quiet me…quiet me. Immediately I feel an indescribable nothingness, a oneness with God. It lasts several minutes.

Sister pilgrim, Theodora, becomes upset in the cave of Francis because it brings back anguish over her brother's imprisonment in the Philippines, along with feelings of empathetic claustrophobia for him. Jim and I had been collecting stones on the Carceri trails for our fraternity back home, and when I pray that I might help Theodora, I feel prompted to give her a stone. I press it into her hand, telling her it will give her peace. After she regains her composure, Theodora tells me she had immediately felt peace radiating warmly from the stone. Praise God in his mercy.

After seeing the caves of Leo and another brother, I sit on a bench looking out over the valley and up at Mount Subasio. I take a picture of the sun peeking through the forest canopy. Birds sing and the wind blows gently. Suddenly it occurs to me why Francis would burrow into a cave to meet God: The beauty of nature can bring God close only to a certain point. Beyond that it is a distraction. One must empty oneself completely to experience God in the depth of one's soul.

In the late afternoon, Jim and I walk the streets of Assisi. The city is ancient, charming and beautiful with its pale stone of warm beiges and rose tones. Because of the 1999 earthquake, much of the mortar is new and lighter in colour than on our previous visit.

Virginia: When I saw the caves where Francis and his brothers prayed and slept, I was deeply touched by their poverty, simplicity and trust in God. I would complain all the time, sleeping in the cold, rocks, rain and snow. In the caves I felt the presence of Francis especially where I spent some time praying and reflecting in one particular cave. In that cave I drew a cross with two hands on the wall. This sign represents that I surrender myself to Jesus to be used as he wants. I felt so comfortable, so in peace that I didn't want to leave this place. One day I hope to come back to Assisi and look back on what I have accomplished since leaving that symbol of surrender to Jesus.

Brother Alan: The morning dawns bright as the mists shrouding Assisi slowly melt away revealing the Spoleto Valley below. Today will be a good day! Although the itinerary says it's a day off, the group has decided to taxi up to Ermo delle Carceri. So we will spend two hours on retreat to Brother Francis' caves on Mount Subasio returning to the guesthouse for a communal lunch and then the remainder of the day will be free. As for now, breakfast and morning prayer before we depart.

The carceri I think has been a mixed experience

for many, yet most did venture to the valley caves! Theodora was emotional afterwards when we left the confines of the Grotto. I heard on the part of David that it was claustrophobia. I suspect that and also it allowed her to somehow touch the reality and soul of her dead brother who died while incarcerated. It is at such moments when we become prayer as opposed to praying.

I have returned more convinced that piety, while part of our faith's expression, is best suited for glorifying and responding to God's glory. Piety does not equal prayer. Prayer is rooted deeper in our psyche and soul. It is the prima facie viaduct through which God speaks to us. Yet this means we must be silent. Therefore if we wish to pray well, we must bring ourselves to a place of silence where we become transformed into the likeness of Francis, Clare and Jesus. Then we are at the beginnings of becoming a prayer.

While at the carceri I found "my" cave. It is located across the ravine on the far side at the end of the trail. There I had come home, home to the place where I had begun my friendship with silence and contemplation in 1999 on July 20th to be precise. There had been many visitors since then, as many anonymous crosses were perched precariously in the niches of the walls, and along the base were a multitude of prayer cards and pictures and postcards with images of Francis on them.

I had left a memento of my previous visit to this

spot but had forgotten what it was. As I slowly and gently began to pick up cards and read them...what a wonderful gift! In my hand I held my card. I had returned to not only my cave but also myself! The writing still visible... "This place is sacred to Brother Alan Gaebel, OFM Cap July 20, 1999".

I did however make one mistake and inadvertently hurt my dear friend, B, whose understandable response was to avoid me for the remainder of the day (upon our return to the guesthouse).

After our lunch together, we all went our ways for the remainder of this day was a free day. I slept after having gone to Santa Chiara with Margaret and then the Roman For a under the Piazza del Commune before the Temple of Minerva.

During the early evening drumming reverberates through the Assisi streets. It's the Assisi drum and flag corps. I love bands having played in the cadets during High School. I cannot resist the urge and leave for the Piazza del Commune to be entertained with rhythmic and synchronized timpani and wonderful flag tossing and twirling exhibitions... I get several wonderful photos.

While on the Piazza I notice B as she slips inside a store as I walk along. Having made eye contact, I know she is avoiding me. I return to the guesthouse to prepare for prayer. But how can I lead prayer with dispute and hurt between B and me? She has arrived after me and again avoids me. I decide to invite her for a walk in the garden.

Thankfully, she accepts and alone with the Spoleto valley and St. Clare's Bell Tower in the background, we, like true Franciscans, begin the journey of reconciliation and peace. I can now stand in the chapel and lead prayer. I give some input on San Damiano and we conclude. My heart at peace, I can now sleep as Assisi begins to hush for the night. The bells of Santa Chiara will toll soon enough a new morning, and after Mass and later lunch, we will head for San Damiano followed by Santa Chiara.

Franciscan Readings
The Rule for Hermitages –
Francis and Clare: The Complete Works, pages 146-147
(A hermitage was a secluded place enclosed by hedges or some natural barrier so that outsiders might not enter. In the ancient monastic tradition, such prayerful isolation was seen as a principal support of the contemplative life.)
Of Francis' devotion to the angels –
Celano, Second Life, CXLIX, 197
Of Francis' devotion to our Lady –
Celano, Second Life, CL, 198

Day 8
Itinerary
Morning Prayer. We will recall St. Clare's early life and admission into Francis' fledgling movement. Like Francis and

Clare in their time, we will walk to the church and Poor Clare monastery of San Damiano. Upon our return to Assisi we will catch our breath and spend time at the Basilica of Santa Chiara where we will visit the Tomb of St. Clare and spend some quiet time before THE Cross of San Damiano.

Pilgrimage Notes

Today is Sunday. At 10:00 a.m. we join the Sisters of Atonement at Mass in the chapel of St. Anthony's Guesthouse. The sisters are so hospitable! Sr. Susan attends carefully to my wheat-free diet. Even at yesterday's special dinner, I was served an alternate to the pasta: a delicious tomato and parsnip dish.

It's a pleasant, sunny day, slightly cooler than yesterday – perfect for visiting San Damiano and Santa Chiara. Although Clare's body lies in the crypt at Santa Chiara, it is at San Damiano that I feel the presence of the saint. We wander through Clare's dormitory, chapel and cloister, awed by the simplicity and sacredness of the place. Francis loved San Damiano, having rebuilt the church himself. Giving it to Clare and her sisters was a gift from his heart.

At Santa Chiara, I remain in prayer before the gaze of the Jesus that spoke to Francis. I long to take a picture of this crucifix which had once hung in the little church of San Damiano. So I furtively snap a couple. One of my sister pilgrims tells me she had taken a "forbidden" photo once and it didn't print. (The pictures do turn out, but they are somewhat faded – pale like my own spiritual vision.)

Virginia: The crucified Jesus at the entrance of San Damiano struck me profoundly. I spent some time just looking at the crucifix and praying before it. The passion of Jesus and his suffering became so real. I could see the agony and pain he went through for our salvation. Later, at St. Clare's Basilica, Virginia "made a promise to go every day and pray in front of the Jesus who spoke to Francis. I made this commitment because I want to listen deeply within to what Jesus is telling me, not just me talking, but listening as Francis did.

Brother Alan: Today we began with our usual breakfast and celebrated with the local house Eucharist. By this time (10:00 a.m.), John Juhl arrived and joined us as a concelebrant. Sr. Sue and I read.

We later went for lunch and gathering at the front gate, left for San Damiano where we stayed for an hour. I particularly still enjoy sitting in the chapel rebuilt by Francis. I doubt that I can get any closer to him than there in that chapel reconstructed by himself. While sitting, I notice Margaret behind me, and I reached over and taking her hand, placed it on the cold stones, telling her that they are the very ones placed there by Francis.

Before leaving, I prepare the group for our next stop for the day, Santa Chiara. I am still utterly impressed by the San Damiano Cross and it holds my gaze for a long time. Although the side chapel is busy with pilgrims and tourists, they fade away as I envision the Cross in the church of San Damiano just 1.5 kilometres below. I notice particularly the glint of gold surrounding Jesus' head in the Byzantine halo. I don't yet know just why. After some time, I quietly leave.

Funny, St. Clare's tomb hasn't really moved me. However, the small display on the other side of the crypt contains the Papal Bull granting her the privilege of Poverty. I am in awe of her struggle, her tenacity and her great desire.

Tonight there will be no evening prayer since I will dine with Brother John at 8:00 p.m. Tomorrow we will visit the valley below Assisi.

Franciscan Readings
Message from the San Damiano crucifix -
Legend of the Three Companions, 13:

One day while Francis was fervently imploring God's mercy, the Lord revealed to him that he would shortly be taught what he was to do. From that moment he was so full of joy that, beside himself for gladness, he would let fall occasional words of his secret for all to hear. This happened in spite of his habitual caution;…His companions noticed how changed he was; and indeed his heart was already far from them, even though occasionally he accepted their company. They tried to probe into his mind and again asked whether he was thinking of marrying, and as before he answered in a figure of speech: "I shall bring home a bride more beautiful, richer, and nobler than any you have ever seen."

A few days after this, while he was walking near the church of San Damiano, an inner voice bade him go in and pray. He obeyed, and kneeling before an image of the crucified Saviour, he began to pray most devoutly. A tender, compassionate voice then spoke to him: *"Francis, do you not see that my house is falling to ruin? Go, and repair it for me."* Trembling and amazed Francis replied: "Gladly I will do so, O Lord." He had understood that the Lord was speaking of that very church which, on account of its age, was indeed falling to ruin.

These words filled him with the greatest joy and inner light because in spirit he knew that it was indeed Jesus Christ who had spoken to him. On leaving the church he found the priest who had charge of it sitting outside, and taking a handful of money from his purse, he said: "I beg you, Sir, to buy oil and keep the lamp before the image of Christ constantly alight. When this is spent I will give you as much as you need.".

Francis restores San Damiano –
Legend of the Three Companions, 24
Clare's early years at San Damiano –
The Little Flowers of Saint Clare, 9
Silence, the Parlour, and the Grille –
Rule of Clare, Chapter V
St. Clare's Christmas Eve –
Little Flowers of St. Francis, 35

Day 9

Itinerary

Morning Prayer. We will recall Francis' conversion and the gathering of the early brothers beginning with Bernard of Quintavalle. We will visit the Basilica of Santa Maria degli Angeli and the Portiuncula. Later upon our return to Assisi we will recall Francis' later life and his reception of the Stigmata. We will also consider two of his favorite hermitages, Monte Cassale and La Celle, as well as introduce St. Margaret of Cortona.

Pilgrimage Notes

Early morning Assisi. Beyond the nearby Church of Santa Chiara, everything is veiled in mist. The sky directly above is blue with wispy streaks of white. Our neighbours down the hall left earlier and noisily. For the past two nights there has been laughter and loud talking between 11:00 and 12:00 p.m. despite an understood silence. Another sound that I have come to recognize is a loud clicking of heels.

On a more pleasant note, soft music floats through the foyer and halls in the early mornings. It wafts through the dining room at breakfast. Today it is the instrumental music from the opera, Madame Butterfly.

This morning's Reading is from James: be merciful, not judgemental; if your faith does not have works, what good is it?

Our first stop today is Rivo Torto. It's hardly a river – more like a trickle. Presumably it held more water in the time of Francis. This was where Francis and his companions first settled after having their Rule approved by the Pope. Here the brothers lived in wattle huts and cared for lepers.

Next we visit the Assisi War Cemetery honouring soldiers who died in World War II. We wander among the tombstones marked with the names and ages of the dead. Most were in their twenties with some in their teens and a few in their thirties. There is a Canadian section where I spend most of my time. Everything is beautifully kept with flowers on every grave. We pilgrims are truly moved.

We visit St. Mary of the Thorns, commonly called the Leper Church since it was built by Francis and his brothers for the lepers. Now privately owned, the little church is rough, small and beautiful in its simplicity.

Finally we enter St. Mary of the Angels which shelters the tiny Portiuncula inside its magnificent walls. I touch the stone with my hands, imagining the holy hands of Francis upon it. The Portiuncula is so tiny, yet Francis was delighted with it. There are lots of people here today. It's difficult to be alone with Francis.

Then I remind myself that in the busy world it seems difficult to be alone with Jesus. But he's always there…waiting for me.

Anna: Everything I visit in Assisi is of great interest to me. Some places are surprising, for example, the cemetery and the private little church. I most enjoyed the places where Francis slept, prayed, and built churches, especially the church of Santa Maria della Spina (in private hands now).

Virginia: Santa Maria della Spina, the leper church, struck me the most. I think of Francis gathering people who were not accepted by the public because of their condition. Not only did he take care of them, but he built them a place where they could express their faith, pray, sing, cry, and share among themselves. By doing this, Francis imitated Christ and responded to the Gospel. I have learned to focus on St. Francis and his great compassion. He was not afraid of these people. I feel more drawn to Francis, and have a strong desire to follow him with my whole heart and try my best to imitate him.

Brother Alan: When our taxis arrive, we are off to our first stop, Rivo Torto, where we spend about 30 minutes. Many are surprised to see just how small this "torrent" is. I answer questions about the replicated huts inside and the site itself. It is hard to make the shift from Franco Zefferelli's "Brother Sun, Sister Moon" to the stark reality of Rivo Torto. Only small mud and wattle huts beside a tiny stream, no caves, no river... yet this is the place!

We pause for another 20 – 30 minutes at the Assisi War Cemetery. This stop has an impact: 49 Canadian boys are buried here below Assisi...the city of peace. As I gaze upon the grave markers, what tugs at me most are the ages...17 to 32 for most. I simply can't imagine it, giving one's life when it's only really beginning. Please God, help us to find and know peace in our time so that this doesn't continue...

We silently (for the most part) move on to Santa Marie della Spina (Our Lady of the Thorns) more commonly known as the Leper Church. I am really excited and pleased to be able to bring my pilgrim group to this site, built by Francis. It is in private hands and not available to most groups.

Finally, we conclude our morning at Santa Maria degli Angeli and the real cradle of our spirituality, La Portiuncula. Although the last time I saw this place it was closed and under construction, I still appreciate that vision. That is what it was, a vision unencumbered with panels and trappings, naked stone much as Francis, the early brothers and Clare would have known. Yet today it still calls out to me. There is a presence at the Portiuncula that I find difficult to articulate.

Certainly there is peace, awe, reverence... but I can also see Francis and Clare, her hair falling on those very stones beneath *that* altar. I can see the dim red orange light of the torches on the walls, and I can see Francis and Clare sitting at their Eucharistic Banquet in the dark under the open sky...It is all so alive and so real. I really don't want to leave this place so *alive* with the presence. And then, just a few steps away, the spot where Brother Francis breathed his last. Just to be able to be here…indescribable.

Later, at evening prayer, we share the day. Much of the sharing is not too deep, save for some reflecting about the War Cemetery. I suspect that today's places and their realities haven't yet processed. No problem. This I know will take time.

Franciscan Readings
Rivo Torto –
Celano, First Life, pages 146-147
The Portiuncula –
Mirror of the Order - Legend of Perugia, 8
Francis bequeaths St. Mary of the Porziuncula to the friars –
Mirror of Perfection, 55

Day 10
Itinerary

Road Trip! By private coach we will visit the Basilica of St. Margaret of Cortona, the hermitages of La Celle and Monte Cassale, and lastly – La Verna itself, the site of the sacred stigmata. At La Verna we will celebrate with prayer and join as friars solemnly process to the site itself in the mid-afternoon.

Pilgrimage Notes

The overcast skies do not dim our excited anticipation as we set out on today's well planned road trip, wearing jackets and carrying bagged lunches prepared by the guesthouse. On this day there are thirteen seculars, one Capuchin brother, one Capuchin priest, one Franciscan Sister of Atonement and two Franciscan Sisters of Mary Immaculate, the latter two using the excursion as part of their orientation to the region.

As we travel through the hilly Italian countryside, I jot down words that come to mind: joy, peace, wonder, fatigue, freedom, emptiness, fear, tension, forgiveness, conversion, repentance, struggle, journey, amazement, humbling, acceptance, student, numbness.

A winding climbing road leads to Cortona, its ancient buildings close to the road. Large, hard rain drops splatter against the bus. All is grey, gloomy and wet when we arrive at a grey stone church in a stark, bare setting. Here lies the body of Margaret of Cortona, first Third Order Secular saint, lying perpetually in state before the altar of her church.

At La Celle the sun bursts through. It is so picturesque! We are treated to a private tour by a pleasant, polite Capuchin. We move in awe through chambers of ancient stone and wood. We admire the choir with its large, beautifully expressive crucifix carved from wood and the grille designed to view the consecration during Mass times. The simplicity of the chapel, refectory, and cell of Francis speaks to our hearts.

Aboard the bus once more, the pilgrims discuss the meaning of pilgrimage. Margaret says that Webster's defines it as a long, weary journey to a shrine. Jim shares his inscription copied from the door of St. John Lateran: "A pilgrimage is a path of conversion, an interior preparation for a renewal of the heart".

I turn my attention to the passing scenery. It has become a beautiful sun-dappled day. Everything seems larger than life. A small, grey lizard runs straight up the wall of a little building. Construction cranes are everywhere repairing buildings large and small. I wonder how much of this work is related to the earthquake. Winding asphalt carries us through wooded mountainous regions. Along the way, we see little stone shrines in remote places, and tiny huts with oval, open doorways.

Monte Cassale is beautiful, charming, inviting and holy. A delightful, cheerful little friar takes us on tour after other friars treat us to wonderful cappuccino. I steal back to the cell of St. Anthony, patron of our home fraternity, with mischievous Teodora who obligingly takes my picture there. Outside we wander by terraced gardens, herbs, vegetables, shrubbery, chickens, goats. We leave feeling happy, fulfilled, and joy-filled. I've taken too many pictures today and only have one left for Mount La Verna.

As we head for the holy mountain, the skies cloud

over and soon showers begin again. The towns we drive through have houses of stone and stucco, tile roofs, and puddles on their streets. The pilgrims talk quietly or nap. It's been a long day, it's 3:00 p.m., and we're still fifteen kilometres from La Verna.

La Verna is drenched with rain. It is huge and bleak, stark and sprawling with noisy hordes of tourists (surely not pilgrims) everywhere. Orange plastic fencing partitions off areas under repair. Workmen, quiet and patient, repair masonry and shovel earth. My first attempt to visit the place of St. Francis' stigmata fails. The chapel and the stairs to it are clogged with people attending Mass. Of all Franciscan places, La Verna receives the most visitors after Assisi, I read.

Later, I return and visit the first cell of Francis, the Chapel of the Stigmata, the cells of Bonaventure and Anthony. They are mercifully free of congestion, and peaceful in shadowy light.

Jim has found a way into the cloisters that he knows I have been wanting to see. Excitedly, he leads me through a chapel door and down cavernous halls. The old cloister. The ancient library. St. Clare's hall. I am stunned by the immense size and barrenness. But it does not speak to me personally. Irritated with the noisy crowds outside, let down by the silent starkness inside, I feel as empty as the shrine's interior corridors. The pure joy I experienced earlier in the day at La Celle and Monte Cassale cannot be rekindled.

As we ride back to Assisi, many nod off. It's been a long day. A rainbow appears in the sky just as on the return from our previous road trip. The sign of the covenant.

Reflecting on the four shrines, the highlights for me were certainly the hermitages. In their isolation and simplicity, they were the richest and the most beautiful physically and spiritually. I hope someday I can give La Verna another chance.

Anna: La Celle. Tranquility reigns there. For me Francis' presence was in the mountainous places. Francis was in the air, among the rustling leaves. In the darkness in the forest, I imagined him trodding to his cell.

Virginia: All the caves I have seen are very special and significant for me. I was blessed to arrive at the La Verna chapel just as the priest was preparing to celebrate Mass. Receiving the Eucharist where St. Francis received the stigmata made me feel so special. In this place, Francis opened himself to the Lord, cried, prayed, suffered, gained strength and came out renewed. I don't think Francis could have survived in these caves without Jesus in his life. But he did it all for the love of Jesus, to give good example and to build his community. La Verna made me realize and focus on my daily prayer and the necessity of personal change and renewal in the manner of St. Francis.

Brother Alan: Today we are up early and off to Tuscany. Two more sisters join us along with Brother John so now we number 18. Our first stop is in Cortona. We visit the Basilica of St. Margaret of Cortona who was the first Secular Franciscan to be canonized.

We travel by bus then for about 15 minutes to La Celle. At first there seems to be "no one home" but after ringing the bell, Brother Pietro arrives. Speaking through Virginia, we are graciously received and taken on a detailed tour including Brother Leo's cell, the Choir and Chapel and the Refectory built by Elias. Everyone seems in awe. It has been a good day so far. Although we have encountered rain…at each of our stops the sky is opened and we are blessed with sunshine.

From La Celle we journey across the Appenine Mountains to Sansepolcro to visit our next hermitage, Monte Cassale. I don't say much about this site since I know the brothers are expecting us. However, we arrive during Pranzo and the bell is unanswered.

So we gather at the visitors' area and enjoy our bagged lunches overlooking the valley vista below. Above our heads grapes hang heavy on an arbour. The setting is idyllic. Afterwards Brother John and I connect with the resident Friars who are finishing Pranzo. One elderly friar, upon realizing we are Canadians, speaks to us in English, and after providing each of us with an Espresso, leaves to open the Church (which is officially closed until 3:00 p.m.).

Then he surprises me by sacrificing his siesta to take us around Monte Cassale in great detail! We have again been truly blessed and are grateful recipients of famed Tuscany hospitality!

After about two hours, we leave and continue our pilgrimage to La Verna! La Verna. Atop the mountain, we are 1200 metres above sea level.

Our prayer experience, however, is muted by the 'tourist' faction and a couple of Italian groups intent on seemingly claiming ownership of the space. Although disappointing and aggravating, I have expected this as a possibility. Our group breaks up and agrees to gather for a 5:00 p.m. departure. Margaret and I fight our way past the crowd to visit the Chapel of the Stigmata where we manage about 5 minutes of relative silence before the next group swarms in. I guess I will *never* understand Italian reverence which to me seems *totally lacking*!

We continue our pilgrimage as we descend to the Projecting Rock, Francis' first cell at La Verna, the small chapel of St. Mary of the Angels with the della Robbias inside, and finally the Basilica itself.

I'm left with the sense that although important, La Verna has been anti-climactic. This isn't uncommon. We often arrive with such high expectations at such sites.

Our journey to Assisi is almost complete as we leave La Verna. Many sleep on the return trip to Assisi. Evening prayer is cancelled in favour of

Morning Prayer.

Franciscan Readings
Second Consideration of the stigmata -
Little Flowers of Francis, II, 2
The crucified seraph –
Celano, First Life, 94 - 95
Francis receives the stigmata –
Legend of the Three Companions, 69 - 70
St. Francis farewell to La Verna –
Once a year, on the evening of 30 September, a letter is read aloud in the refectory at La Verna. It is the letter in which Brother Masseo handed down the very moving "Farewell to La Verna" uttered by St. Francis on his final departure from the Holy Mountain (30 September 1224). In commemoration of this date, which also marks the celebration of the Feast of St. Jerome, doctor of the church, the religious, in honour of that saint, include his name in their prayers during the daily

----

Day 11
Itinerary
We will recall Francis' death and burial and its meaning for us today. We will visit the three churches which make up the Basilica of St. Francis, and celebrate Eucharist among the final resting places of Francis and his first brothers. In the evening before retiring we will celebrate the Transitus.

Pilgrimage Notes

Again this morning I see the lizard that lives on the lower terrace. Green and quite large, he walks casually across the stone walkway.

Early this morning Bach is playing quietly. Then the music shifts to Celtic strains, and a piper plays a slow, plaintive 'Danny Boy', bringing tears to my eyes.

Today is the first anniversary of the September 11 attacks on the New York towers and the Pentagon. At Morning Prayer, Brother Alan points out that our Eucharist this afternoon in Assisi time will coincide roughly with 9:00 a.m. American time, the time of the original acts of terrorism. Moreover, our Mass will be held in the Basilica's private Peace Chapel.

We tour and pray in the wonderful Basilica of San Francesco. We gaze upon the ancient frescoes in the lower and upper churches. How very fortunate we are to be here in this holy place. I present our Fraternity's petitions in the crypt at the tomb of Francis. Then an additional blessing, thanks to Brother Alan's influence! We are permitted within the Sacro Convento. In delighted silence, we walk along wonderful old corridors, pass the cloister, and attend mass in the Peace Chapel.

For the second time since arriving in Assisi, I hang laundry in the lower garden. It's so peaceful and beautiful here that this simple task becomes a prayer.

At Night Prayer, we celebrate the Transitus. Brother Alan has arranged seven candles in the form of a cross. Afterwards we share the day's experiences and thank Brother Alan for being so caring and available to our endless needs. Many speak of making changes in their lives. Conversion, the daily calling.

Virginia: I was in Assisi four years ago immediately after the earthquake. At that time, we were only allowed to visit the tomb of St. Francis. I remember how I knelt at the altar of the tomb and wept and wept. This time at the tomb, I am reminded of how connected I felt to Francis and Jesus. Like Francis, I open myself totally to Jesus. After I left the Basilica, I felt renewed. The Basilica of St. Francis spoke to me on the life and death of St. Francis. St. Francis spoke to me and touched me deeply.

Brother Alan: It is September 11. We gather for Morning Prayer, remembering the tragic events of a year ago. When we celebrate Eucharist at the same local time as the attacks took place in New York City, I hope the significance isn't lost. Otherwise, today is a free day until we gather for evening prayer.

This afternoon I have the privilege of a tour through the Conventuals' "Franascanum" located between the Piazza del Commune and the Basilica di San Francesco along Via San Francesco. It is an amazing array of corridors and has three exceptional chapels. And also the Franciscan Centre for Ecumenical Dialogue for Peace which is part of the

Conventuals' Assisi-based ministries! Thanks to my Brother John's involvement in an Italian language course here in Assisi, this tour was through one of his classmates.

Tonight's prayer is our final liturgy. I am happy to hear of realizations of the need for spiritual growth and of occasions of spiritual growth among the group. I feel very touched and am grateful for their presence without which none of this experience would have been possible. The expressions of thanks and gratitude are deeply moving and humbling.

Deo Gratias!

Franciscan Readings

Bro. Alan's Notes: *The tomb of St. Francis.* After numerous unsuccessful attempts to find the actual tomb, it was finally discovered in January 1818, after fifty-two nights of digging. The body was found beneath three heavy blocks of travertine, where it had been hidden by Brother Elias some 600 years before. In 1230 Pope Gregory IX ordered the small passageway leading to the funerary cell walled in so that the body could not be stolen and transported to some other place. Leo, Rufino, Angelo and Masseo are buried around the tomb of Francis.

The Lower Church. Frescoes on the vault of the transept are by an unknown painter of the school of Giotto. Above the altar are others of the same school exemplifying poverty, chastity, obedience, and the triumph of Francis. Cimabue painted St. Francis;

Lorenzetti, the *Madonna del Dito* and the *Crocefissione*.
In the upper church along the nave, under the gallery, is the famous series of twenty-eight frescoes depicting the life and miracles of Francis by Giotto and his pupils (1290-1295).

Among the relics found here are: *the original bull of Honorius III approving the Rule*, and the *blessing written to Brother Leo* in Francis' own handwriting.

Letter of Brother Elias (on the occasion of Francis' Death) - *Introduction:* Saint Francis died somewhat late in the afternoon of Saturday, October 3, 1226. A great crowd gathered from all the country about Assisi. Thomas of Celano describes how the Friars spent the entire night in prayer. On the next day, the body was taken with great solemnity to the little church of St. George in Assisi, where the burial took place. After the funeral services, Brother Elias, the Vicar over the Order, sent to all the Provinces of the Friars Minor an announcement of the passing of St. Francis. Historians are of a mind that this classic encyclical letter was quickly composed, probably by the following Wednesday, and that copies were speedily made and duplicated to all the Provinces.

In this message Brother Elias seeks to console the Friars whose father has been taken from them. He wishes to point out that, despite the pressure of their loss, there is even cause for joy, because, before his death, the Saint had blessed all his sons and had forgiven them all their faults against him, whether these were in word or thought or deed. Thereafter he announces the great privilege of the Stigmata in the body of their father who was, as it were, crucified.

This letter is written in the manner prescribed by the

rhetoric of the time. It abounds in quotations from, and in reference to, passages of Holy Scripture. Sometimes there are as many as six in one sentence. There is also possibly a line taken from a popular medieval poem and what may be a reference to a sermon of St. Bernard. [Taken from: EARLY FRANCISCAN CLASSICS. Serra Press, St. Anthony's Seminary, Santa Barbara, CA, 1954. Private Printing. P.122]

Letter of Brother Elias - *Omnibus of Sources*, Appendix III

Day 12

Itinerary

Morning Prayer. Today is a "Free Day". This is a good opportunity to return once again to those places in and around Assisi which spoke to your heart or perhaps enkindled your Franciscan vocation. General discussion.

Pilgrimage Notes

Our last full day in Assisi is a 'Free Day'. We pilgrims hardly know what to do or see. Every minute, every second is so precious. We wander the little city saying good-bye in our hearts to the sacred stones lining the streets and compiling the ancient buildings. There is a spiritual magnetism in this holy place. The earth itself exudes energy, wisdom, history. I am so conscious that I walk in the footsteps of Francis, Clare and their many relatives and companions!

Jim and I take a final stroll of the lovely gardens of St. Anthony's Guest House. The guesthouse had been severely damaged in the earthquake, but like so much of Assisi, has been faithfully and lovingly restored.

At noon we eat in a restaurant called Tavola Calda Dal Karro. We sit by a window enjoying the breeze. Later we buy cheese and meat for evening munching. As we return to the guesthouse, I take a final picture of a group of Mother Teresa's Sisters of Mercy in front of Chiesa Nuova.

On behalf of all of us, Margaret has bought a gift for Brother Alan to show our immense appreciation of his planning, devotion and care.

Oh! How I hate to say good-bye!

Brother Alan: A final free day! Dave, Virginia and Bette Ann are off to Florence. Margaret is visiting Santa Chiara this morning. The others are continuing to explore Assisi. I have done my final laundry before packing, and will have lunch with Margaret and Ann.

Sometime today I will have to conclude our business dealings here at the guesthouse and get to Daca for those Tau crosses…

It has been an easy morning and while the warm Assisi sun and gentle breezes dry my laundry, I have walked to Daca and purchased my Taus for St. Francis Table. For the remainder of my day I will simply relax and check on the sights and sounds that are Assisi today. As I do, I find myself giving thanks to God for Brother Francis and Sr. Clare, for Assisi then and now, and for the Brothers and Sisters who have through their presence made this pilgrimage the exceptional and spiritual experience that it has been. My heart sings Alleluia!

A great afternoon with Margaret who, on behalf of the pilgrims, buys me a gift, so I select two St. Martin's colorful paintings. Later, Brother John and I finally visit San Pietro below the hill, near the gate of the Basilica di San Francesco.

Franciscan Readings
Chapter of Mats –
Little Flowers of Saint Francis, 18

Day 13
Itinerary
Travel by private coach to Rome, arriving back at Casa Il Rosario. Evening Prayer. Arrivederci Assisi…

Pilgrimage Notes

As we take leave of St. Anthony's Guesthouse, one of the dear sisters gives us each a tri-fold prayer card. On it is their Patronal Prayer to Our Lady of the Atonement and other guardian saints, the Threefold Salutation to Mary, the Memorare, Ejaculations on

Leaving Chapel, Prayer of Francis when in a Church, Unity Prayer and the Prayer for Peace.

We drive to Rome in two vans. En route, I have the opportunity to converse at length with Beatrice. Beneath her unassuming quietness, she is a woman of faith and courage who has endured many trials and challenges. How little we know about our creature earthlings! Each one has a heart, a soul, a story. Everyone deserves our respect, consideration and prayers.

After a brief nap at Casa Il Rosario, Jim and I return to St. Peter's Basilica, spend some time in prayer there, and visit the Treasury. Later we enjoy a leisurely evening meal and decide to take a long walk through Rome. Although we soon realize we are lost, we continue on. The back streets of Rome have many secrets. Lovely courtyards are hidden within plain alleys. Gateways provide glimpses of pleasant inner laneways. Numerous elegant apartments are concealed behind austere walls, permitting sightings through an occasional unshuttered window.

At night between 9:00 p.m. and midnight there always seems to be entertainment in Rome. On our first night here, almost two weeks ago, there opera coming from somewhere, and the second night we heard band music. Tonight on our way back to Il Rosario, we pass an open courtyard where a movie is being projected on a wall. People sit around on benches and on a central fountain. Perhaps this is the entertainment courtyard.

As I prepare for bed, I reluctantly acknowledge that we are now in rapid transition from pilgrim to tourist.

Anna: I had to go back to St. John Lateran, and I did so this afternoon. Of all the places I visited, this church made the greatest impression on me because I felt I had arrived home.

Brother Alan: Back to Rome! Upon our arrival some of our group catch up on sleep. As for myself, I join Simone, Marcel, Margaret and Beatrice as they make their way to the Coliseum. This time they are early enough to get inside. After a tour, and while waiting for our small group to gather, I manage to complete my gift shopping!

Once gathered, we take a taxi to San Giovanni di Laterno. I take them on a tour including the Baptistry built by Emperor Constantine. Then we make our way across the street to the Santa Scala , the sacred steps allegedly brought back to Rome from Pilate's Praetorium in Jerusalem.

When we left the Coliseum, Beatrice had *insisted* that she would walk back to Il Rosario where we are staying. I remember thinking to myself, "She is going to get lost." We return by cab from San Giovanni in Laterno, intending to go out for dinner. However, on our return it is evident that Beatrice *has not* returned.

My worst fears realized, I am becoming quite angry with Beatrice's saying she understands when in fact she doesn't. Yet, as we prepare to form a couple of groups to walk back to the Coliseum...we learn that the police have phoned and Beatrice is coming home by taxi.

As I leave the guesthouse, who is walking up the street?...but Beatrice as if nothing had happened!!! On one hand I could strangle her but I am so glad she is back I cannot be angry with her. I remind myself of her age at 82, and am somewhat in awe of her "street smarts" in a foreign country and city! (Even I am still learning.)

After this, we all enjoy a wonderful Chinese dinner and return to our guesthouse grateful that our lost sheep is home, and call it a night!

Franciscan Readings
Francis blesses Assisi –
Legend of Perugia, 98-99
Clare on the grace of working –
Rule of Saint Clare, Chapter VII
Clare on poverty –
Rule of Saint Clare, Chapter VIII

Day 14
Itinerary
Morning Prayer. Today is a good time to visit any sites in Rome which you haven't yet seen or to return to a favorite one!

Re-pack your luggage and prepare for our friends at airport security and customs for tomorrow we go home

Pilgrimage Notes

At 6:30 a.m., I lie awake listening to the sound of nuns at prayer. Their intermittent singing carries through the building. Off in the distance, church bells ring. Their distance is a contrast to the enveloping bells of Assisi which, beginning at 7:00 a.m., are always close by.

The alley below our windows echo loudly. Voices laugh and sometimes shout. A dog barks. Motor scooters roar between cars, and garbage trucks clank and bang. But at 7:00 a.m. singing and chanting floats across the lane, probably from another convent. Rome is the epitome of contrasts!

After breakfast, Jim and I try to devour Rome by bus and foot. We stop in churches, including the Church of Maria above the Medina. We admire the Pantheon's granite columns and massive dome, visit the baroque Trevi Fountain, and linger on the Spanish Steps. We enter the Hassler Hotel where we are courteously told that for security reasons we cannot leave the lobby. Apparently we have not been mistaken for their normal clientele.

On the Number 40 bus, Jim and I both have our shoulder bags unzipped by young women who, fortunately for us, are thwarted by the warning yells of other passengers! We are astonished at their deftness because we were being especially vigilant.

After all, Jim already had his wallet stolen on Day 2 of this pilgrimage on this very same bus.

We have seen others of these "gypsies" at church entrances, on various buses, and on the streets. Young women often have a baby at the breast, while older women are bent and clinging to canes. Even though the set-ups are probably staged, one cannot help but feel pity. And who, I wonder, is minding the toddlers and other children while all this is going on?

On this last evening in Rome, a helicopter circles the area at length. What is it doing? Is it looking for something...someone? Looking from my window, I try to see it, but it remains tantalizingly out of my sight. In the streets below, residents, visitors, cars, scooters and taxis come and go.

Again there is chanting and singing across the way. I lean out my window and read "Residence S. Pietro" on a stone address block a few doors down. I have seen young women come and go from this building. This must be the source of the singing and chanting I sometimes hear drifting down the via. These lovely prayers float heavenward from its windows, as they do from Il Rosario, blending beautifully with the sounds of everyday life.

It stirs the heart to be reminded that spirit-filled communities, much like these, dot mother earth. I feel especially blessed to belong to the global Franciscan family, and to have such dear friends among its members.

Brother Alan: Today dawns bright and clear. It is our final day in Roma and I am going to fulfill my promise to Margaret and escort her to some of the remaining sights (with Beatrice in tow).

We begin by taking a taxi to the Pantheon which we explore. Then we walk a short distance to Santa Maria sopra Minerva to view Michelangelo's "Risen Christ," we attempt to locate Il Jesu but discover Chiesa San Ignatio, the Church of St. Ignatius Loyola instead.

This turns out to be providential since there is a shrine to St. Margaret Mary, Margaret's baptismal saint! We walk from there to Fontana di Trevi where after tossing our coins in and taking the requisite photos, we stop for an enjoyable lunch.

After lunch we make our way to the Piazza di Spaghre, the Spanish Steps. Margaret had mentioned her desire to see them when we first mentioned this pilgrimage. I had decided that if she came with us, I wasn't going to let her see Rome without seeing them.

After resting a short while, we set out for the Piazza Barbrini. I manage to overshoot our street and we stumble onto the Palazzo Quinale…Again, since we are there, we take some photos and then walk back to our intended destination, the Piazza Barberini along Via Quattro Fontone, the street of the four fountains which we see along the way.

Arriving at our destination, we find the Church of the Immaculate Conception closed. With a half hour to wait, we enjoy a gelati across the street in front of a well shaded café. Once opened, we tour the church more commonly known to Capuchins as "The Bone Church". Over 4000 Capuchin friars are in pieces, various parts of skeletons stacked in piles or used as decoration in various crypts. A whole new reality for the term "Rest in Peace."

I find it curious and funny: Relic worship gone amuck. However, for me it is an important sight since St. Felix of Cantalice is entombed in the church sanctuary upstairs.

Upon concluding our final visit, we take a taxi home. Having packed and repacked, I make my final entry as I prepare to glean some little sleep before we meet our bus at 5:00 a.m. We will (I hope) arrive at the airport around 6:00 a.m., check in and then catch our flight to Milano.

Franciscan Readings
Clare's farewell to Francis –
Legend of Perugia, 109

Day 15
Itinerary
We will travel by private coach from Casa Il Rosario back to Rome's Fumicino Airport to connect with our flight back to Toronto.

Pilgrimage Notes

We will travel by private coach from Casa Il Rosario back to Rome's Fumicino Airport to connect with our flight back to Toronto. Pilgrimage has been described as exterior mysticism while mysticism has been considered internal pilgrimage. Living and praying in and around Assisi blesses one with a vivid impression of the places inhabited by the brothers and sisters of Francis. I pray that I can include some elements of internal pilgrimage in my remaining life journey.

St. Francis was in the world but not of it. The Gospel was his guide. This is the model for our own journey. As did Francis, we must continually strive to balance prayer and solitude with service to others. So challenging a task becomes more manageable when we join our prayer with others. This reminds me that I have completed the joyful assignment of presenting the petitions of my fraternity brothers and sisters to Francis and Clare. How fortunate I have been to personally visit the tombs of the holy founders!

Anna: Looking back on these last few days, I believe I got to know Francis best at La Celle. And walking along the path in the Carceri, I came to appreciate the sacrifices he made to follow Christ and leave us a legacy. At the onset of this pilgrimage, I had no expectations apart from reacquainting myself with Assisi. However, I have been given the gift to reflect in future months on the spiritual benefits of this journey. Pax et Bonum.

Virginia: As a secular Franciscan, I have never prayed directly to St. Francis but to Jesus. But this pilgrimage has made me focus, pray, and love St. Francis more and more. It was like I met him for the first time. His presence was everywhere. He spoke to me in different ways. I am really grateful for St. Francis because he is to me like a second Jesus. He suffered in order to build his community and to be an instrument of peace, love, and justice. He gave us wonderful examples to follow and never forget.

Brother Alan: After a brief wait of one-and-a-half hours, we are on our way home to Toronto! Deo Gratias! A fine pilgrimage successfully concluded.

Franciscan Readings
Solitude versus Preaching –
Little Flowers of Francis, 16

Rules of Francis' Family

Part I:

THE WAY OF LIFE

FIRST ORDER

Chapter 1: The Rule and Life of the Friars Minor is this, namely, to observe the holy Gospel of our Lord Jesus Christ by living in obedience, without property, and in chastity. Brother Francis promises obedience and reverence to his holiness Pope Honorius and his lawfully elected successors and to the Church of Rome. The other friars are bound to obey Brother Francis and his successors.

SECOND ORDER

Chapter 1: This is the form of life of the order founded by blessed Francis, called the Order of Poor Sisters, which form is to observe the holy Gospel of our Lord Jesus Christ by living under obedience and without property and in chastity. Clare, the unworthy handmaid of Christ and the little plant of the most blessed Father Francis, promises obedience and reverence to the Lord Pope Innocent and to his canonically elected successors, and to the Roman Church. And as in the beginning of her religious life, she with her sisters promised obedience to blessed Francis, so now she most faithfully promises to obey his successors. Also the other sisters shall always be bound to obey the successors of blessed Francis, and they must likewise give obedience to Sister Clare and to the other abbesses canonically elected who shall succeed her.

THIRD ORDER REGULAR

Chapter I, 1: The form of life of the Brothers and Sisters is this: to observe the gospel of our Lord Jesus Christ, living in obedience, in poverty and in chastity. Following Jesus Christ after the example of Saint Francis, let them recognize that they are called to make greater efforts in their observance of the precepts and counsels of our Lord Jesus Christ. Let them deny themselves (cf. Mt 16,24) as they have promised the Lord.

THIRD ORDER SECULAR

#4: The rule and life of the Secular Franciscans is this: to observe the gospel of our Lord Jesus Christ by following the example of Saint Francis of Assisi, who made Christ the inspiration and the centre of his life with God and people. Christ, the gift of the Father's love, is the way to him, the truth into which the Holy Spirit leads us, and the life which he has come to give abundantly. Secular Franciscans should devote themselves especially to careful reading of the gospel, going from gospel to life and life to the gospel.

Rules of Francis' Family
Part II:

POVERTY

FIRST ORDER

Chapter 6: The friars are to appropriate nothing for themselves, neither a house, nor a place, nor anything else. As strangers and pilgrims (1Pt 2,11) in this world, who serve God in poverty and humility, they should beg alms trustingly. And there is no reason why they should be ashamed, because God made himself poor for us in this world. This is the pinnacle of the most exalted poverty, and it is this, my dearest brothers, that has made you heirs and kings of the kingdom of heaven, poor in temporal things, but rich in virtue. This should be your portion, because it leads to the land of the living. And to this poverty, my beloved brothers, you must cling with all your heart, and wish never to have anything else under heaven, for the sake of our Lord Jesus Christ.

SECOND ORDER
Chapter 6: My sisters and I have been ever solicitous to safeguard the holy poverty which we have promised the Lord God and the Blessed Francis, so, too, the abbesses who shall succeed me in office and all the sisters are bound to observe it inviolably to the end: that is to say, they are not to receive or hold onto any possessions or property acquired through an intermediary, or even anything that might reasonably be called property. It is however permissible to hold as much land as necessity requires for the integrity and the proper seclusion of the monastery; and this land is not to be cultivated except as a garden for the needs of the sisters.

THIRD ORDER REGULAR
The truly poor in spirit, following the example of the Lord, live in this world pilgrims and strangers (Mt 10, 27-29). They neither appropriate nor defend anything as their own. So excellent is this most high poverty that it makes us heirs and rulers of the Kingdom of heaven. It makes us materially poor, but rich in virtue. Let this poverty alone be our portion because it leads to the land of the living. Clinging completely to it let us, for the sake of our Lord Jesus Christ, we shall never want anything else under heaven.

THIRD ORDER SECULAR

#11: Trusting in the Father, Christ chose for himself and his mother a poor and humble life, even though he valued created things attentively and lovingly. Let the Secular Franciscans seek a proper spirit of detachment from temporal goods by simplifying their own material needs. Let them be mindful that according to the gospel they are stewards of the goods received for the benefit of God's children. Thus, in the spirit of "the Beatitudes", and as pilgrims and strangers on their way to the home of the Father, they should strive to purify their hearts from every tendency and yearning for possession and power.

Rules of Francis' Family
Part III:

VIRTUOUS LIVING IN
THE COMMUNITY

FIRST ORDER

Chapter 10: With all my heart, I beg the friars in our Lord Jesus Christ to be on their guard against pride, boasting, envy and greed, against the cares and anxieties of this world, against detraction and complaining. Those who are illiterate should not be anxious to study. They should realize instead that the only thing they should desire is to have the Spirit of God at work within them, while they pray to him unceasingly with a heart free from self-interest. They must be humble, too, and patient in persecution or illness, loving those who persecute us by blaming us or bringing charges against us, as our Lord tells us,

"Love your enemies, pray for those who persecute and calumniate you" (Mt 5,44). "Blessed are those who suffer persecution for justice' sake; for theirs is the Kingdom of heaven" (Mt 5,10). "He who has persevered to the end will be saved" (Mt 10,22).

SECOND ORDER

O my sisters, I admonish and exhort you in the Lord Jesus Christ to beware of all pride, vainglory, envy, covetousness, care and solicitude for earthly things; eschew utterly all backbiting, enmity, murmuring and strife, always striving to preserve among yourselves that unity of spirit which is the bond of peace. Let not the unlettered be anxious to learn, but rather let them consider that, above all else, they should desire to possess the Spirit of the Lord who works all wisdom. Be humble, prayerful, pure in heart, patient in time of sickness and adversity. Love them that hate you, and pray for them that despitefully use you, for the Lord says: "Blessed are they that suffer persecution for righteousness' sake; for theirs is the Kingdom of heaven; and again, you shall be hated by all for my name's sake, but the one that perseveres to the end shall be saved."

THIRD ORDER REGULAR

Chapter 5, #20: Let the sisters and brothers be gentle, peaceful and unassuming, mild and humble, speaking respectfully to all in accord with their vocation. Wherever they are, or wherever they go throughout the world, they should not be quarrelsome, contentious, or judgmental towards others. Rather, it should be obvious that they are joyful (cf. Phil. 4,4), good-humoured, and happy in the Lord as they ought to be. And in greeting others, let them say: "The Lord give you peace."

THIRD ORDER SECULAR
#17a, #18, #19: In their family they should cultivate the Franciscan spirit of peace, fidelity, and respect for life, striving to make of it a sign of a world already renewed in Christ. Moreover they should respect all creatures, animate and inanimate, which bear the imprint of the Most High, and they should strive to move from the temptation of exploiting creation to the Franciscan concept of universal kinship. Mindful that they are bearers of peace which must be built up unceasingly, they should seek out ways of unity and fraternal harmony through dialogue, trusting in the presence of the divine seed in everyone and in the transforming power of love and pardon. Messengers of perfect joy in every circumstance, they should strive to bring joy and hope to others. Since they are immersed in the resurrection of Christ, which gives true meaning to Sister Death, let them serenely tend toward the ultimate encounter with the Father.

ABOUT THE AUTHOR

Gloria Pearson-Vasey lives in a picturesque Ontario town with her husband, one of their four sons and a menagerie of sorts. Her background includes nursing, psychology, music, journalism and theology. She enjoys reading, travelling, nature, and time spent with family.

Gloria writes in various genres reflecting her eclectic interests and obsession with research. Visit her website gloriapearsonvasey.com to read her blogs and more about her books.